TODAY...

… an Encouraging 7/70 Journey
Hebrews 3:13
Journey 2

Sandy Picek

Prodigal Publishing
Denton, Texas

Copyright 2020 Sandy Picek

PRODIGAL PUBLISHING

Published by Prodigal Publishing

ISBN: 978-1-7355383-4-1
Printed in the United States of America

Cover Illustration photo by: Sandy Picek

For the many who inspired these stories, the Holy Spirit who guided these writings, God my Daddy who loves me, and Jesus who saved me.

What you hold in your hand is what I call "a 7/70 journey with Jesus." It is a different type of journal, or journey, that you can walk through for 70 days and only 7 minutes a day. This is the 2nd of the Journey Series books.

Every Journey Date has a true-life story, along with encouraging words from God.

There are 70 "journey dates" and at the end of each story, there are 3 questions to think about. You can jot down how something on a given day has touched your heart or impacted you.

We are told, *"But encourage one another daily, as long as it called Today, so that none of you may be hardened by sin's deceitfulness."-* Hebrews 3:13. My hope is that you will be encouraged by these stories and feel the touch of Jesus as you read them.

Blessings over you today!

Joyfully in Him,
Sandy

Journey Date 1 _____

I started a new job and my husband, and I had to do some renovations and moving around of things, because one of the blessings of this new job is that I got to work from home. However, in the moving of everything my computer died. My husband is a computer guru, but we were also facing other situations. Two weeks after I started my job, Bill had to have an unexpected hernia surgery. Then two weeks after that we discovered our 15-year-old kitty, Chicago Girl, had severe diabetes and was not doing well. Then Bill started having chest pains to find out that his left descending bypass that he had five years previous, collapsed and he had a couple of blocked areas. So, he had stints put in. I didn't even know that a bypass could collapse or that a stint could be put in a bypass, but I guess they can.

The reason I am sharing all of this is not for sympathy or the poor me thoughts, but it's made me think about patience through the trials. If you are reading this, then you qualify as one of the people who have been in the multitude of trials and waiting. Waiting for the results from a doctor. Waiting for the shoe to drop at work to determine if you are in the next group to get laid off. Waiting to find out if the one you love so much is going to walk back through the door after facing a war on the streets or a war across the world. Or even waiting and wondering if by chance, you will be able to wake up the next day and forge through the deep waters of anxiety and depression. I know all these things. Been through all of these things, and the one thing that I do know for certain… is that I don't know what tomorrow holds, but I do know who holds it!

Peter talks about standing through the trials, and what we gain, in Chapter 1 – vs.6-9 *In all this you greatly rejoice, though now for a little while you may have had to suffer grief in all kinds of trials. These have come so that the proven genuineness of your faith—of greater worth than gold, which perishes even though refined by fire—may result in praise, glory, and honor when Jesus Christ is revealed. Though you have not seen Him, you love Him; and even though you do not see Him now, you believe in Him and are filled with an inexpressible and glorious joy, for you are receiving the end result of your faith, the salvation of your souls."*

Today, sweet friend of Jesus, do not be discouraged. This place that we live in, the bodies that carry us, they are all temporary. The trials are just a passing of time that will bring us closer to Him here on earth. But oh the glory that we will encounter one day, will wipe away all tears, fears and discouragement.

****

ASK YOURSELF:

What is God revealing to me today?

_____
_____
_____
_____
_____
_____

How do I see God working in my life today?

_____
_____
_____
_____
_____
_____

What can I do to bring a blessing to someone else?

_____
_____
_____
_____
_____
_____

Journey Date 2 _____

We had so much rain in the month of May. I noticed how incredible everything looked. Our rose bush has become a rose tree, standing over eight feet tall. The flowers tripled in size and the grass continued to grow so fast that I could barely keep it cut. As I look at the beauty of nature, I see a freshness and newness of the growth of things. I see new buds of life appearing in the flowers and on the trees. I see the clouds forming that bring down the rain. But the best part of the rain is the rainbow. After the rain falls and the sun shines the most beautiful sight is to see a rainbow. Do you remember the last time you saw a rainbow? How do you feel inside when you see one? Does it have the effect of "Wow", that overcomes you.

I realized that "WOW" feeling is God revealing His promise one more time. He tells us in Genesis 9, "*the rainbow is My reminder to Myself and to you that I have made a covenant with you, to never leave you, and that you are My creation.*"

You are HIS creation. He is delighted in you and sees the beauty in you that He created. He wants you to know that you are valuable to Him, and He will stand in the covenant with you forever.

Today, may the Lord pour down on you a ray of sunshine in your eyes and a rainbow over your head.

****

ASK YOURSELF:

What is God revealing to me today?

_____
_____
_____
_____
_____
_____
_____
_____

How do I see God working in my life today?

_____
_____
_____
_____
_____
_____
_____
_____

What can I do to bring a blessing to someone else?

_____
_____
_____
_____
_____
_____
_____
_____

Journey Date 3 _____

I love to walk outside and feel a cool wind blowing and smell a freshness in the air. Even though you can't see the wind, you know it's there because you can feel it. Sometimes we can have "windstorms", which can cause all kinds of problems. Branches broken from trees, antennas ripped off houses and shingles flying through the air. We know there is wind because we do feel it, and we see the "power" of the wind when it comes as a storm. But to try and actually grab a piece of wind is not possible.

We must remember the wind because it is a creation of God. It is one thing that we cannot see, but we feel. Yet the wind is like our Lord. I know that I cannot reach out and physically touch Him, like I can touch my husband, but I can feel Him and know His presence is all around me, like the wind.

As human beings, we like to "feel" and "see" things. But sometimes, we are asked to have faith and believe, that God does have everything under control and trust what we cannot see. His Word tells us, *"While our minds are not on the things which are seen, but on the things which are not seen; for the things which are seen are for a time; but the things which are not seen are eternal."* 2 *Cor. 4:18*

When our faith and hope is placed in the unseen hands of God, we are given the freedom to let Him take care of us, because He is forever and eternal.

Today, as the wind blows across your skin, think of God, and speak softly into the unseen place of His heart, and let Him cover you with His mercy and peace.

****

ASK YOURSELF:

What is God revealing to me today?

_____
_____
_____
_____
_____
_____
_____
_____

How do I see God working in my life today?

_____
_____
_____
_____
_____
_____
_____
_____

What can I do to bring a blessing to someone else?

_____
_____
_____
_____
_____
_____
_____
_____

Journey Date 4 _____

This past Spring, I planted several flowers in pots and hanging baskets. As Summer approached the flowers grew and they bloomed, and they grew some more. Then, the blazing sun started to shine down, and the heat was upon us, and the flowers. Though I kept watering (most of the days), the heat was too much for a couple of my plants, in particular one hanging basket with petunias. I finally took the basket down from its hanging post and set it on the ground. It was dead! Every stalk of flower was black and burnt. I kept watering the other plants and apparently some of that water must have sprinkled into the dead basket. You see I noticed a green sprout coming up out of the dirt. At first, I thought it must be a weed, but as the days have passed it is actually a flower stalk. There was a beautiful purple flower beginning to bloom. How in the world could that little flower have grown out of that dead and burnt basket? I imagine it was the sprinkling of the water that gave new life to a dead seed.

Sometimes I feel like that basket of flowers... burnt and nothing left to offer. Burnt by circumstances out of my control. Burnt by the challenges and trials of life. Jesus tells us in John 5:21 - "For as the Father raises the dead and gives life to them even so the Son gives life to whom He will."

God gives us a sprinkling of life through His Son, Jesus. If you are standing in drought or facing a dry and burnt place in your life, the Father will raise you up and give you life. Let Him rain down on you today for a fresh drink.

Enjoy the sprinkling of Him today!

****

ASK YOURSELF:

What is God revealing to me today?

_____
_____
_____
_____
_____
_____
_____
_____
_____

How do I see God working in my life today?

_____
_____
_____
_____
_____
_____
_____
_____
_____
_____

What can I do to bring a blessing to someone else?

_____
_____
_____
_____
_____
_____
_____
_____
_____

Journey Date 5 _____

Wow, I don't really know where to start. Like everyone else in our world, we were all frozen in time to see the multitudes of people in pain and suffering from such an event as Hurricane Katrina. Some days I just sat and cried because my heart ached for the pain of people that I don't even know. Picture after picture, story after story, we kept hearing of the devastation… yet I knew somewhere amid this tragedy, there had to be a triumph. I keep asking myself, "can I see it?" "What is the victory of all of this?" How can ANY good come from such horrific images?" Then I silently I heard God speaking to me, "Sandy, I am the same God I was the day before the hurricane, and as I am right now. – Do you trust me?" My thoughts were immediately to those who lost their lives and didn't know Jesus Christ as their Savior – now they will never have the chance to make the choice to know Him…. And my heart wept. And I hear Him again, "Sandy, I am the same God, do you trust Me?" Then I want to ask the question "Why, Lord? – Why?" and once again, the same small voice,

"Sandy, I am God, I am the Alpha and the Omega – I AM the Beginning and the End, and now it is up to My chosen children to share about what MY beloved Son did… He too died, and I saw Him die, and yet I loved Him more than anything else. I knew that if He didn't take up the cross there would be no forgiveness. There would be no unconditional love. There would be no place to run to and lay your burdens down. And there would be no one to hold your hand in the time of death. Now is the time to tell everyone about the love that Jesus has for each person. Go and tell the world that I AM God, and that He IS the way to healing. Remember, John 3:16? … For I so loved the world that I gave MY ONLY begotten Son, that whoever believes in Him will not perish, but have eternal life." " Many now walk with me and are dancing in the streets of Heaven … bring more into the kingdom that we may all one day live forever in the glorious place of Heaven."

I pray today that God inhabits every part of your being and brings a new revelation of who He is to you.

****

ASK YOURSELF:

What is God revealing to me today?

_____
_____
_____
_____
_____
_____
_____
_____

How do I see God working in my life today?

_____
_____
_____
_____
_____
_____
_____
_____
_____

What can I do to bring a blessing to someone else?

_____
_____
_____
_____
_____
_____
_____
_____
_____

Saturday morning, I got up before my family awoke, and I went outside to sit on the patio and just "veg" out and "talk to God". It was a beautiful, cool morning. The sun had risen, the wind was blowing slightly, and the temperature was around 60 degrees. It was just about as perfect as it could be, especially for Texas. Occasionally a strong wind would blow thru, and I could hear something like a group of people applauding. I looked around trying to figure out where that sound was coming from. Then it would go away. Sure enough a strong wind would blow through and there was the sound again. As if hundreds of people were clapping their hands together. I looked again – couldn't see anything. Finally, I asked, "Lord, where in the world was this sound coming from?" All of a sudden the wind blew stronger again, and the clapping was strong and loud and continuous. So, I turned quickly to look to the street behind me and aha! – there it was, two 20 foot plus, tall Cottonwood trees, clapping their leaves together. The stronger the wind blew, the louder the clapping was. It truly sounded like hundreds of people clapping.

Now the strange thing about this, is that when I first went and sat on the patio and I was talking with God, I was asking some direct questions to God. Very personal questions, questions that dealt with risky decisions, questions that I needed to know if I was heading in the right direction. There HE was, once again, in the wind, clapping, applauding, saying "yes" go that way. Every time I asked a risky question, He always answered with an applause of the clapping of the leaves.

Applause or clapping is such an outward show of how we feel. When we clap our hands we show our approval, our appreciation, our love, and our excitement. I love to worship God, Jesus and the Holy Spirit with singing, clapping and raising of my hands. I know HE loves for us to worship Him. God was doing the same to me on Saturday morning. He wasn't worshiping me, but He was applauding me for asking Him for direction. I found a verse in Isaiah that blew me away – God tells us, "For you shall go out with joy, and be led out with peace; The mountains and the hills shall break forth in singing before you, and all the trees of the field shall CLAP THEIR HANDS" – Isaiah55:12

Isn't that something, He already wrote about His trees clapping for us. "WOW! – Thank you, Lord, for loving us so much!"

I pray today that you can hear God's applause. Sit out on your patio, and just listen to Him. He is there.

****

ASK YOURSELF:

What is God revealing to me today?

_____
_____
_____
_____
_____
_____
_____

How do I see God working in my life today?

_____
_____
_____
_____
_____
_____

What can I do to bring a blessing to someone else?

_____
_____
_____
_____
_____
_____
_____

Journey Date 7 _____

Have you ever had anyone tell you, "Happy Valentine's Day!" The more I think about Valentine's Day, the more it saddens me. Sounds kind of strange, doesn't it? To show love, there will be thousands upon thousands of people who will be sending or receiving flowers, candy, stuffed animals, jewelry, cards, all kinds of "sweet" gifts. If I am a betting person, I bet my husband will get me something for Valentine's Day, because that is the kind of person he is.

What saddens me is that so many people seem to wait until this day to express their love for someone else. Why do we wait until Valentine's Day to say those magical words "I love you?" Why can't it be an everyday thing, or at least a once-a-week thing? For some people I guess it is easier to show love than for others to show love. I must confess that I was not the best person to tell someone "I love you", but as time has gone on, I have realized how important it is to share those words with people that you do love *AND* to share the actions that go with them.

That is why we are so blessed, because we have a God who loved us so much that HE sent HIS Son to take on our sins, burdens, guilt, pain, and heartache. I must write the very familiar passage: "For God so loved the world that He gave His one and only Son, that whoever believes in Him will not perish but have eternal life. For God did not send His Son into the world to condemn the world, but to save the world through Him." – John 3:16-17

Oh beloved, I hope you know today that you are loved. I don't know where you stand, or what you believe in, or who you believe loves you… I am here to tell you that God truly loves you. He also sends his children throughout the earth to share that love with each other. So today, if no one else tells you those words, then I will… "I love you!" You are a blessing.

Today I hope you realize how special you are and how loved you are.

****

ASK YOURSELF:

What is God revealing to me today?

_____
_____
_____
_____
_____
_____
_____
_____

How do I see God working in my life today?

_____
_____
_____
_____
_____
_____
_____
_____

What can I do to bring a blessing to someone else?

_____
_____
_____
_____
_____
_____
_____
_____

Journey Date 8 _____

Okay, I hate to admit what I am about to admit… but I think
EVERYONE will have to confess to this one. It's about the milk
carton that sat on the refrigerator shelf just a little too long (or a lot
too long) and the milk becomes thick and curdled and looks like
cottage cheese. Yep, you know what I am talking about – at some
point in your life you've probably done it at least once. The worst
part about this is that you must open the carton and pour the curdled
milk down the drain, and when you take the milk cap off the
carton… OH MAN what a smell!!! The smell is so bad even your
dog runs away from the kitchen. I know some of you are giggling or
thinking, oh, I am so glad I am not the only one that does that.

Then there is other experience of food in the kitchen. The one that
captures the nostrils of the dog, the cat, the kids, and even the
neighbors next door… home baked cookies. I would even go as far
to say the cookie dough in the package counts. YOU have to cut and
slice the dough and when it is cooking the yummy, cookie aroma is
so WONDERUFL! The smell will wafer out into the living room,
through the hallway into the bedrooms and here comes the family,
wanting to know what kind of cookies are being baked. It is one of
the most capturing smells around.

Did you know that being a follower of Jesus Christ is being like that
cookie with that wonderful aroma? In 2 Corinthians 2:15 Paul
writes, "For we are to God the fragrance of Christ among those who
are being saved and among those who are perishing." It is because
of Ephesians 5:1 & 2 that you are that aroma. "Therefore, be
imitators of God as dear children. And walk in love as Christ also
has loved us and given Himself for us, an offering and a sacrifice to
God for a sweet-smelling aroma." Every day you live, you leave
that sweet fragrance everywhere you go. When someone feels like
they have just opened their "soured milk" of life and they have to
dump the "curdles" down the drain then they, or we, truly want to
replace that with something wonderful and sweet smelling. We have
all been in the curdled places of life… you may be there right now. I
tell you today that God wants to unleash that sugar cookie smell
inside of you.

Today, look around you and take a deep breath… smell the beauty of God that surrounds you and let Him cut and slice the dough and pop it in the oven and watch what happens in your life.

****

ASK YOURSELF:

What is God revealing to me today?

_____
_____
_____
_____
_____
_____
_____
_____

How do I see God working in my life today?

_____
_____
_____
_____
_____
_____
_____
_____

What can I do to bring a blessing to someone else?

_____
_____
_____
_____
_____
_____
_____
_____

Recently, my daughter was stung by a wasp while at work. She was preparing meals in the kitchen for her residents. While plating a meal, a wasp landed on her hand. She felt something tingle, then she looked down and saw the little fellow. She knew she was stung but kept on working not thinking much about it. A little time went by and one of her co-workers came in. Katy started telling her about the wasp. Her co-worker looked at Katy's hand and realized it was starting to swell. She told Katy to keep an eye on it. Another 15 minutes or so go by, and she noticed Katy's hand was turning black where the wasp stung her. The resident nurse was called to come and look at her hand. By the time the nurse arrived the place had swollen, and the black was traveling down her hand. They determined she was probably allergic, so she was sent to the ER. It was approximately 3 hours from the time of the sting until the time she saw the doctor. At the time she was treated her whole hand was swollen, and the black had stretched across her hand. The spot where the wasp stung her had become a deep black hole. She never knew that a little bit of poison could cause such a mess. She was given a shot, and a dose of Benadryl and was told to go home and rest.

Amazing how quickly that little sting grew into something so big. And where in the world did the wasp come from? Our life can be something like this as well. We just go along, working, living, minding our business, just doing the day to day that we do. Then suddenly BAM, something has "stung" us. What was it? Where did it come from? How did we get in *this* situation? Our relationships with each other, family members, co-workers, even our relationship with God can all of sudden be poisoned by something that seem so small and insignificant. Speaking for myself, most of them time it is usually some words that happen to come out of my mouth that aren't the most uplifting words. Psalm 140:3 says it like this – "They make their tongues as sharp as a serpent's; the poison of vipers is on their lips." The words that we speak can be a poison to someone's heart and soul, and we might not even realize it, until the day comes when we see the "black hole". Or you may be the person that has had the "poison" enter into your life, and you feel like you are being swallowed up. Take heed my friend, God always throws the life preserver when we need it most.

Today, my prayer is that God would release in you a freedom from the poison. Whether you feel you are the giver or receiver, or even both, it doesn't matter, God is standing right there. Let Him take your pains and aches.
****

ASK YOURSELF:

What is God revealing to me today?

_____
_____
_____
_____
_____
_____
_____
_____

How do I see God working in my life today?

_____
_____
_____
_____
_____
_____

What can I do to bring a blessing to someone else?

_____
_____
_____
_____
_____
_____
_____

Our eyesight is one of the most precious gifts that God has given us. I know this even more today, as I have acquired a new pair of progressive trifocals. It has been interesting and challenging to get adjusted to these new "eyeballs". In some ways, I didn't realize how bad my vision really was. Some things were very blurry, (especially my reading), but some things were only a little distorted or fuzzy. With the trifocals, my vision is much clearer with the fuzzy things, but the reading part is a whole different story. When reading, I find that I need to adjust my eyesight to focus completely on one spot and move my entire head to follow along on any given sentence. This is a whole new technique of reading and is quite challenging. It is not natural for me to have "tunnel vision", as it may seem, but I know in the long run my brain will become accustomed to the different "eyeballs", and my overall vision will be much clearer.

What seemed so profound to me was when I was driving to church on Easter Sunday. It was the day that we go to church and remember not the death of our Savior, but to recall God's unfailing love for us by giving us a living Savior. A Savior that forgives, disciplines, embraces, gives hope, and loves us unconditionally. How truly amazing this Easter story is. Yet, there were those who were walking along the Road to Emmaus, who came upon Him, after He had risen from the tomb, but could not "see" Him. How could the men who walked side by side with Christ, not recognize Him? How could they even carry on a conversation with Him and not know that it was Him? They had become so distraught over their loss and pain in their lives that their "vision", or mindset, could only think in a "tunnel vision" way. They had no concept that Jesus was walking and talking with them. Their minds were full of other things that got in the way of the one true goal, and that was to see Christ Himself. Yet as this part of the Easter story was read from Luke 24: 13-33, my eyes were opened a little more.

As I sat with my new glasses on my face, my precious husband leaned over to me and could see I was having some difficulties, and simply said, "you are still getting adjusted to your glasses, aren't you?" It was so simple and clear - I was letting my fears of wondering if I would ever get use to reading with the new glasses, or getting headaches from the new glasses, get in the way of my thinking of how my "vision" should be. It will take a couple of weeks or so for my brains and eyes to get adjusted to working together. I know there are many who already have mastered wearing the trifocals and their vision is clear. This is how we should be with our relationship with Christ. When we can't see past our tunnel vision, and life happenings seem to keep getting in the way, the focus needs to be moved to a clearer picture. We need to feast our eyes upon our Lord and remember that He is our refuge and our fortress.

Whatever your vision is focused upon, whether it is financial loss, physical pain, relationships broken, concern about employment, hearts that are heavy, envy of a co-worker, doubt about your children, critical illness, wherever your focus is, turn your eyes to Jesus, and lay it before Him. He will surely meet you on the Road to Emmaus.

Today beloveds, believe that He Has Risen, and that your Road to meet Him is short. He is walking right beside you, longing to hold your hand.

****

ASK YOURSELF:

What is God revealing to me today?

_____
_____
_____

How do I see God working in my life today?

_____
_____
_____
_____

What can I do to bring a blessing to someone else?

_____
_____

Journey Date 11 _____

Have you ever lost anything? Have you ever been on a trip
somewhere and left something behind? Or you planned a trip to be
somewhere, and you got where you were going and realized you left
something at home that you desperately needed? I imagine the
answer would be yes from most of us. I have done all three of
these. Just this past weekend I was staying in a hotel, and I had
taken my jewelry off and laid it on the bathroom counter. My
jewelry consisted of a pair of silver hoop earrings, a pearl ring that
my daughter gave me, a Sylvester watch (yes, that is Sylvester the
cat) and a ring that I inherited when my mother passed away. Well,
the next day came, and we got up, got dressed, left to go to our next
destination. We hadn't been there more than five minutes and my
heart sank.... You guessed it, I left my jewelry sitting on the
bathroom counter at the hotel. I wasn't too concerned about the
watch and earrings, but both rings meant more to me than just being
a ring. They were "heirlooms" to me. How could I have done such
a ridiculous thing? What was I thinking? Didn't these "things"
mean more to me than just jewelry? Of course, they did but that
doesn't mean I left them there on purpose. As a matter of fact, I was
so excited to be able to see an old friend that day, that I just wanted
to get where we were going and didn't even think about the jewelry.
But when I realized what I had done, my heart just sank. I ran to
where Bill was and told him what I had done. He immediately
called the hotel and he said he would drive back and pick up my
jewelry. I waited for Bill to come back, and I prayed. I asked God
to please watch over these special things and to remember how
"invaluable" and important they were to me. A little while later Bill
walks in with the jewelry. I thanked him and thanked God for taking
care of me in my time of "senselessness".

Immediately God was showing me that we do the same thing with
Him. We will be going along and know that God, the Holy Spirit,
and Jesus Christ are with us everywhere we are. Life then gets
BUSY, and very filled up and we keep going on the paths that seem
so crazy and chaotic that we just leave Jesus behind. Then we begin
to feel that feeling of "oh no, I've lost Him… how do I get Him
back, where can I go look for Him?" Unlike the jewelry in the hotel,
I don't think I remember the places that I have left Jesus behind.

Also, unlike the jewelry in the hotel, when I do leave Him behind, he will not stay there. The jewelry couldn't follow me, but God gives us a promise in Deuteronomy 31:6 and Joshua 1:5… "I will never leave you or forsake you." Isn't that too grand! We can walk away from God, (or try to), but HE will not walk away from us, OR stay sitting on the counter. I tell you today, if you have felt like there is no way for you to reach out to Jesus, or that you have gone on a trip so far away that He couldn't find you, it is absolutely not true. Just stretch out your hand to the sky and let Him touch you today. He is the "heirloom" of your life, and He wants to be worn in your heart.

God is standing there right next to you… just slip Him on your finger and feel His touch in your heart.

****

ASK YOURSELF:

What is God revealing to me today?

_____
_____
_____
_____
_____
_____

How do I see God working in my life today?

_____
_____
_____
_____
_____
_____

What can I do to bring a blessing to someone else?

_____
_____
_____
_____
_____

Journey Date 12 _____

Mornings can be so beautiful. The sky is still dark, and the temperature is dropping to around 68 degrees. There is a cool breeze blowing, and everything just feels right. Do you ever have those mornings? Everything just feels good, and right? I know of several people who have gotten up believing just that... and then they head off to work only to find out that they are being laid off. Or that the company they are working for is moving to another location, and no one is going to the new place. With today's economy, and unusual circumstances happening in our governmental offices, it can be a scary thing to wonder every morning, "will I have a job today"? I am learning that my job is not definite. Anything can happen, and I may be unemployed tomorrow. The hard part about having a job for any length of time, is that we sometimes take the job for granted. Does that make sense to you? Almost as if there is a "silent assurance" that the job will never go away, and that the only way the job will disappear is if "we" make it happen and leave the job.

You probably know someone who has lost their job due to circumstances "out of their control". One thing that I have learned over time, is that anything can change. Not just a job, but marriages, children, health, wealth, and friendships. Any of these and so many more, can become out of our control, even if we think we have that silent assurance. The only thing that I know that never changes, and never waivers is the love that our Lord has for us. Jesus speaks openly about His love for us and our love for Him in John 15:9-11 - " As the Father has loved Me, so have I loved you. Now remain in My love. If you obey My commands, you will remain in My love, just as I have obeyed My Father's commands and remain in His love. I have told you this so that MY joy may be in you and that your joy may be complete."

During the unstable, everchanging life around us, if we love Jesus, He promises to love us. The job may go away. The marriage may fall apart. The child may turn away from truth. The friend may move away. The bank account may be empty. BUT... His love is never empty and always remaining with you. Whatever the situation that you are standing in today, whether it is a "feel right" moment, or an "out of control" moment... Jesus is standing there right next to you, holding out His arms, ready to love you.

Today, remain in Jesus, and let His love pour over you.

****

ASK YOURSELF:

What is God revealing to me today?

_____
_____
_____
_____
_____
_____
_____
_____

How do I see God working in my life today?

_____
_____
_____
_____
_____
_____
_____
_____

What can I do to bring a blessing to someone else?

_____
_____
_____
_____
_____
_____
_____

Journey Date 13 _____

This past week while driving, I saw at a distance a single vulture feasting on some unfortunate animal. I wondered why there was only one vulture. Usually when there is one, there are tons. As I got closer, I could see what "unfortunate animal" it was. A skunk! This single vulture was standing right in the middle of the dead animal. It was as if the vulture was making a stand, while eating his prey, that the skunk was his, and it would be only his feast. As I kept driving, the waft of horrendous smell from the skunk came trickling into my car. That was some horrible smell. My immediate thought was, "no wonder none of the other vulture's want a piece of this animal, it is absolutely awful." This one vulture was on his own, standing in the middle of this grotesque smelling skunk, and I imagine that the vulture was beginning to smell like the skunk. Could it be that the other vultures did not want a part of the scene? The other vultures not wanting to be around this one vulture because it was beginning to smell as bad as the skunk?

Obviously, we don't know the answer to these questions, but it made me think about us as human beings. How we fall prey to others around us, and become so entrapped with their ideas, or their ways, or their desires. We can stand right in the midst of a crowd, or an individual, that may have a "horrible smell" (words, actions and beliefs) and we don't even know that it is a bad place to be. Like the vulture, the wrong place or person can start to rub off on us, and we begin to "smell" like them. We can become stuck or feel bound in that place. God's desire for us, is that we would learn and grow and "stand in the midst of Him", so that we can become more like Him. When we are more like Him, we have the ability to be free and "unstuck". Galatians 5:1 says it like this... "It is for freedom that Christ has set us free. Stand firm, then, and do not let yourselves be burdened again by a yoke of slavery." You see when we "stand in Christ" we are set free from the "horrible smell" and then God gives us a new scent in Him.

Today, you may be standing in a place that you walked into weeks, months, or years ago, that may seem harmful or uncertain. You may want to move closer to Christ but feel that there is no way out. It is possible to take the step toward His presence, and He will always come and stand next to you, bringing you love, peace and freedom, and the new aroma of Christ.

****

ASK YOURSELF:

What is God revealing to me today?

_____
_____
_____
_____
_____
_____
_____
_____
_____

How do I see God working in my life today?

_____
_____
_____
_____
_____
_____
_____
_____

What can I do to bring a blessing to someone else?

_____
_____
_____
_____
_____
_____
_____
_____

Journey Date 14 _____

How do you react when you go to see a sporting event? We usually are cheering on our favorite team, we yell out things like, "you can do it", or "we need a touchdown", or "you can strike that guy out", and so on. We watch the coach give instructions to the team players, and hope that they are wise instructions. Then, when "our team" scores, it is as if the skies open and the clapping and whistling and shouting could be heard on the next planet. THEN, if our team wins, we walk away with a great satisfaction. Almost like a joy to know that "we" stood by and cheered the winning team. We will stand and cheer and raise our hands in the air, clapping and shouting, to let the coach and the team know we support them and believe in their ability to win. It really is a very gratifying feeling to be part of a winning team.

I don't know about you, but I really do like to associate myself with the winning team or the winning coach. Sometimes though I forget that in the game of life, there can be winning moments, and as believers in Christ we **are** on the winning team. And of course, we certainly have the best coach around, whose name is Jesus. He leads us, teaches us, and corrects us if we don't follow through with "the play" that He has for us. Sometimes, it seems when we stand and clap and shout and raise our hands to our "life coach", we may feel embarrassed, or uncomfortable. Like the coach on a football team, or a baseball team, Christ loves for us to show Him how much we are satisfied with Him being the leader. Many scriptures tell us "Clap your hands all you nations, shout to God with cries of joy, Sing to His Holy name!" (Psalm 47:1, 66:1, 95:1, 100:1)

Today, know that you are on a winning team, the best team of life, and don't forget to tell your "Coach", thank you, thank you, thank you. I guarantee that He will show you how much He loves you, when you show Him how much you love Him.

****

ASK YOURSELF:

What is God revealing to me today?

_____
_____
_____
_____
_____
_____
_____
_____
_____
_____

How do I see God working in my life today?

_____
_____
_____
_____
_____
_____
_____
_____
_____

What can I do to bring a blessing to someone else?

_____
_____
_____
_____
_____
_____
_____
_____
_____

Journey Date 15 _____

One evening I was sitting at a red light, at an intersection. I looked up and it appeared that someone or something was walking across the overpass. I couldn't tell if I was imagining things or really seeing someone. It was dark and a little drizzly, so I thought this could possibly be me still getting use to my glasses. Peering through the windshield, my eyes now completely focused on that moving figure, it was finally clear. A man was walking, carrying a very large backpack. It looks kind of like the one that my son uses in the Army. HUGE! The backpack was about half the size of the man, which distorted the outline of his body. He walked for a few yards and then stopped and would turn and look back over his shoulder. Then he would walk another few yards and turn and look back over his shoulder. It was intriguing and mesmerizing, watching this unusual shape of a shadow walk down the highway. I couldn't take my eyes off him. Each time he stopped to turn around, my mind began to ask questions..."I wonder where he is coming from", "I wonder where he is going", "does he know where he is going?", "why is he walking in the dark?", "what is in that huge back pack?", "are all of his belongings in that back pack?", "why does he stop every few yards and look behind himself?", "is this a journey he is on, or is it an escape?" Well, the red light stayed red long enough for this figure of a man to fade into the darkness, but those questions were still running through my mind.

While driving to the place I was headed for, I felt a need to pray for this man. Then it seemed as if Jesus was sitting next to me answering all my questions. "My dear child, that man is a small representation of this world. So many of My people are wondering in the dark, stopping occasionally to see if their past is following them. They carry a huge burden on their back, most of the time too heavy to bear. The journey here on this earth is short and temporary, though it may seem long and dark. A day will come when those that hear My voice will walk out of their darkness into the light."

I arrived at my destination thinking about this man, and what I felt the Lord was sharing with me, and these passages opened up... I Peter 2:9 - "But you are a chosen people, a royal priesthood, a holy nation, a people belonging to God, that you may declare the praises of Him who called you out of darkness into His wonderful light." & Psalm 91: 4 & 5 - "He will cover you with His feathers and under His wings you find refuge; His faithfulness will be your shield. You will not fear the terror of night, nor the arrow that flies by day..." Wonderful isn't it!? We, you, and me, are a chosen people, WE are a people belonging to God, who will be our shield and take us through our deepest fears and darkness. Oh, how easy it is to forget when the world keeps dumping on our shoulders. How easy it is to pick up the burdens of family, work, friends, and church. But He wants to give you refuge.

Today dear Blessed one, as you walk down those dark roads, remember these words... You are called out of darkness by the blood of Jesus. He is standing right next to you, right now, wanting to hold you up, and keep you covered by His wings. Let him take your burden for just a moment, and rest in Him.

****

ASK YOURSELF:

What is God revealing to me today?

_____
_____
_____
_____
_____

How do I see God working in my life today?

_____
_____
_____
_____

What can I do to bring a blessing to someone else?

_____
_____
_____
_____

Journey Date 16 _____

Some people say that they aren't afraid of anything. I would say at this point in my life I don't consider myself to have too many fears. But something happened this past week and fear snuck in the door. It was about a situation with a friend, and I almost let it get the best of me. I was afraid that if I confronted the situation with my friend that they may not want to speak to me again. Or the fear that I would offend them, or worse, hurt them. Then over the weekend I faced my fear with my friend and had such great relief. It was as if someone took 1,000 pounds off my shoulders. The crazy part about this fear, is that I thought I might jeopardize and destroy a lifelong friendship. But, instead, I believe it drew us closer together. I have shared this acronym before, but I feel that I should share it again. F.E.A.R. = False Evidence Appearing Real. The fear that was consuming me, turned out to be a blessing in disguise. Then I realized that's all fear is - a disguise.

Our pastor was preaching on the fear of God. To fear God is not the same kind of fear that I described above. The fear of God is to recognize, have accountability and willingness to "hear" God. God does not dress Himself up in disguises to have people follow Him. He does not instill the "False Evidence Appearing Real" fear. He desires us not experience "F.E.A.R.". He desires for us to face our fears and lay them at His feet. I love what 1 John 4:18-19 says - "There is **no** fear in love. But perfect love drives out fear... we love because He first loved us."

Do you have a fear today that is consuming you? Until something happens it is false evidence appearing real to you. Face the fear, but don't face it alone... walk beside the F.E.A.R. with the Father and watch how the disguise will disappear.

Today, whatever fear you may be facing, know that you are not facing it alone. As you read this, I pray that God's blessings and peace will poured upon you.

****

ASK YOURSELF:

What is God revealing to me today?

_____
_____
_____
_____
_____
_____
_____
_____
_____

How do I see God working in my life today?

_____
_____
_____
_____
_____
_____
_____
_____
_____

What can I do to bring a blessing to someone else?

_____
_____
_____
_____
_____
_____
_____
_____
_____

Journey Date 17 _____

We have stray cats who get free meals at our house, then we discovered that we have another "friend" eating the food. We left our main door open, and had the screen door closed, so that we could enjoy the beautiful sunshine. As evening came along, my husband, walked over to close the door, only to see two large black eyes staring at him. He was so shocked by the animal, he just stood there for a moment, then started telling me that I needed to come and see what he was looking at. Sure enough, there was a huge raccoon, probably 25 to 30 pounds, sitting on the porch. He was enjoying the "free food". We had noticed over the past few weeks that the food we were putting outside kept disappearing rather quickly. When we I first started feeding the kitties, the food would last two or three days. Now the food was disappearing within hours of us putting the food in the bowl. The cats were still thin, so we knew that they couldn't have been eating all of it, but we just couldn't figure out where it was going. Now we know. The raccoon looked at us like he "belonged here". He did jump to the bottom of the stairs, as more of the family came to the door, but he really seemed perturbed, and that he really did not want to leave. This was *his* patio, *his* food, *his* stake out... and now he was caught. Though the raccoon left, I have a feeling he will probably be back. Raccoons are known to continue to invade and return to their "sights of fulfillment", which are usually places where they can get a "free meal".

Believe it or not, we can have "raccoons" in our personal lives. There may be something that has crept into your life of which you didn't even know was there. Slowly but surely that "thing" keeps sneaking in. You don't even realize that the feeling, the thought, the habit, the past, the "raccoon", whatever it may be, is "sitting on your porch". Then a day comes when that "sneaky thing", is no longer sneaky, but has taken up residence in your life. It has invaded and continues to invade and feast on your heart, mind, and soul. You may not realize that there is a "raccoon" in your life... then again, you might know exactly what I am talking about. One of my favorite passages is Psalm 139... "Oh Lord, You have searched me and You know me. You know when I sit and when I rise; You perceive my thoughts from afar... You are familiar with all my ways

...You have laid Your hand upon me ... Search me, Oh God, and know my heart ..."

Today, God already knows about the "raccoons" in your life because He knows you so well. Turn over whatever may be hindering you from moving forward, whatever may be "eating your lunch", whatever is consuming your mind, whatever that thing is that has crept back into your life, and let the Lord refill your bowl.

****

ASK YOURSELF:

What is God revealing to me today?

_____
_____
_____
_____
_____
_____
_____

How do I see God working in my life today?

_____
_____
_____
_____
_____
_____
_____

What can I do to bring a blessing to someone else?

_____
_____
_____
_____
_____
_____
_____

While I was staying in a hotel, and the sun was setting, I decided I was ready to crash after a long day. While lying in bed I heard this banging noise. It sounded like someone was repeatedly hitting a wall. A loud thud, then a pause, then a loud thud, then a pause, over and over again. I wondered who would be making such a noise? Sleep finally crept in, and the noise went away... until morning. It started all over again, but it was more sporadic. Now I was determined to find out what was making the noise. It sounded like it was around the windows. I opened the curtains, and I saw nothing, and the noise was gone. I thought maybe I was just dreaming all of this up. An hour or so went by and the noise is back. To my surprise I saw the cause. Big black crows were flying into the windows. Head on, hitting them at full force. Over and over these two crows kept flying into the window. As I watched them, I figured out why there were doing such a thing. The windows of the hotel had reflective glass on them. The crows probably saw the blue sky, the clouds and even an image of another crow (really themselves) and they would fly right into the window. They thought what they saw was real... but they were being deceived and believing the deception! I felt bad for the crows. I really wanted to give them a boost to the top of the hotel so that they would stop ramming their bodies into the wall. I could only imagine that there was pain each time they hit the window.

Are you the same way? Are you being deceived by something or someone and continue to follow that direction? Maybe you feel like you are in a rut and can't get out of the vicious cycle. Possibly the reflection or image that you see, feels like a reminder of an ugly past or a difficult present. There can be pain felt each time the reminder is in front of you. I tell you the truth, when you look in the mirror, and see your image, remember this, from the beginning of time... "God created man in His own image, in the image of God He created man; male and female. He created them, and God blessed them." – Genesis 1:27, 28 ... Did you get that? YOU, are created in GOD's image. When you look in the mirror, you don't have to look at the pain or problem, just look at yourself and see God. See His goodness, His love, His mercy, His grace, His forgiveness. See the beautiful creature that HE created – you!

Today, ask yourself this question… "what is that image or reflection that you would like to see changed?" Then, look again and make the statement … "I am a reflection of God, all that He is, and all that He wants me to be."

****

ASK YOURSELF:

What is God revealing to me today?

_____
_____
_____
_____
_____
_____
_____
_____

How do I see God working in my life today?

_____
_____
_____
_____
_____
_____
_____
_____
_____

What can I do to bring a blessing to someone else?

_____
_____
_____
_____
_____
_____
_____

Journey Date 19 _____

I have been very thoughtful of our country and what is about to take place with the leadership and what has already taken place. I thought about the words of our past Presidents and how they talked about the enemy of our country and of this world. Then as I was reading, God placed two scriptures in front of me.

"Be self-controlled and alert. Your enemy the devil prowls around _like_ a roaring lion looking for someone to devour." - 1 Peter 5:8 and "The weapons we fight with are not the weapons of the world. On the contrary, they have divine power to demolish strongholds." - 2Cor. 10:4

I started thinking about my enemy. As the word states, the devil (enemy) prowls around "like" a roaring lion. If you study the habits of lions, you will find that the oldest lion is the one with the loudest roar. He will sit on one side of a clearing and the young lions will wait on the other side, waiting for the "loud roar". Then the prey will hear the "loud roar" and run in the opposite direction and run into the very trap the old lion has set. Yes, the lion may sound and be a powerful foe, but I also think of him as old and toothless. As I pondered the idea of my enemy being "like" a lion and "not" a lion, it made me realize that our enemy likes to roar loudly hoping to paralyze God's children with fear so that we might run right into the very traps we are trying to resist. Traps for us could be, fear of success or fear of failure. It could be the fear of the unknown or fear of being alone.

Have you ever felt like you were prey to something? Do you feel like today you are the "food" for the lion? That is where the second part comes in... "The weapons we fight with are not the weapons of the world..." You have the Lion of Judah on your side. God **IS** the Wise Lion, roaring and fighting for the weak. When you are in a battle zone or feel like "food" and are about to be devoured, remember God's word is powerful. Call out to the Lion of Judah, HE can accomplish anything on your behalf.

My hope for you today is that you are not in fear of an enemy who has no power but stand in faith of the power of your Savior!

****

ASK YOURSELF:

What is God revealing to me today?

_____
_____
_____
_____
_____
_____
_____
_____

How do I see God working in my life today?

_____
_____
_____
_____
_____
_____
_____
_____
_____
_____

What can I do to bring a blessing to someone else?

_____
_____
_____
_____
_____
_____
_____
_____
_____
_____

Journey Date 20 _____

Isn't it amazing today how we can communicate with each other and how quickly we can get messages to someone. Lan lines (these use to be the rotary dial phones), Cell phones, Instant Messenger, Facebook, Texting on cell phones... and I am sure there are many other ways that I have not listed here. I must admit that when I see my adult children texting on their cell phones, with their fingers just flying across that little alpha pad on their phones, I wonder, how did they learn to do this so quickly. And of course, there is a new dictionary of abbreviated words for texting. (I think I know about six of them.) Recently, I began to wonder if we had lost the art of "real communication"... then I heard a story...

A friend of mine had surgery. In the process of preparing at the hospital for his surgery, he became a little nervous and afraid. Then as he was heading to the final stages of preparation, the physician stopped and asked, "would it be okay if I pray for you and this surgery?" My friend said "yes, that would be great." After the doctor prayed, my friend described a feeling of such peace over him. The fear and anxiety had gone away. It was as if there was an instant relief in his body and soul and he knew everything would be okay. He said that is seemed this doctor had a direct line of communication with God, and God heard the prayer.

You see even with all the great, fast, new-fangled ways of communicating today, there is still the greatest way to communicate to the greatest being ever. Prayer. God. Jesus. What more can be said. He is just waiting for you to talk to Him. Jesus tells us in John 15: ..."I have called you friends...You did not choose Me, but I chose you. I appointed you that you should go out and produce fruit and that your fruit should remain, so that whatever you ask the Father in My name, He will give you...." Jesus makes it clear here, when we follow God's voice, He hears our voice. Don't misunderstand what I am saying, God hears our prayers, but that doesn't mean that all answers are what we think they should be. Sometimes we don't understand the answers... but He does want to communicate with you and me. He watches us daily waiting for us to "dial His number".

Today I pray that your phone line to Heaven is ringing off the wall. Bless you dear one!

****

ASK YOURSELF:

What is God revealing to me today?

_____
_____
_____
_____
_____
_____
_____
_____
_____

How do I see God working in my life today?

_____
_____
_____
_____
_____
_____
_____
_____
_____

What can I do to bring a blessing to someone else?

_____
_____
_____
_____
_____
_____
_____
_____
_____

Journey Date 21 _____

Imagine yourself in a vast place that is so immense and full of life. A place like a concert where there are thousands of people all around you. Then suddenly, the lights go out and it is pitch black. You are there, feeling totaling alone. All the people that were around you are gone. You are in the darkness, not one glimmer of light around you. You can't see anything or anyone. You can't hear anything or anyone. You wonder "how long will I have to stay here?"

And out of the darkness, in the far away corner there is a tiny glimmer, almost like a match being lit, and your eyes become completely focused on that tiny light. You walk toward it, thinking if you do, it will lead you out of the darkness. The closer you get the brighter the light gets. You become more focused, searching for the "escape door". You just want out of the darkness. You continue to walk toward the match light. It becomes more like a flashlight, then like a beacon light... you stay completely focused... when you reach the light it engulfs you and you stand covered in light and you can see the door, you can see the pathway to the "outside". You forget the dark that you were standing in and you go forward.

Psalm 18:18 tell us that "He comforts me in the dark and will be my guide." (paraphrased). If you are standing in a dark place whether it is physical, emotional, mental, or financial, HE is holding up the match to guide you. Focus on the match...
you will be bathed in His light.

I pray His blessings upon you today.

****

ASK YOURSELF:

What is God revealing to me today?

_____
_____
_____
_____
_____
_____
_____
_____
_____
_____

How do I see God working in my life today?

_____
_____
_____
_____
_____
_____
_____
_____
_____

What can I do to bring a blessing to someone else?

_____
_____
_____
_____
_____
_____
_____
_____

Journey Date 22 _____

My house needed a deep cleaning. The feather duster was working hard, along with the Windex, and towels. But the vacuum cleaner was a whole different story. My vacuum is a bagless vacuum. This means you can see the dirt, and whatever else gets vacuumed up, in the vacuum cylinder. Once the cylinder is full, it is easily removed, emptied and then you keep on going. As I was vacuuming though, the cylinder never had dirt in it. Now I don't consider myself to be obsessively compulsive about cleaning, so there should have been something in the cylinder. I checked the spinner bar, it was working. Then I checked the hose that was directly attached to the motor, it was clear, so why wasn't this thing picking up any dirt? I asked my handy husband to check out the vacuum. He checked the cylinder, the spinner bar, the connecting hose to motor and he found the same thing… nothing. So, he sat for a minute, looking at all the pieces, and decided to blow through the secondary part of the hose. This part of the hose was the suction to the cylinder. If there was no suction, there was no vacuuming. Sure enough, he blew as hard as he could, and no air came out. After a few moments of poking and prodding at this curvy part of the hose, the culprit was released, and Waa-la… the vacuum was doing its thing again and working like it was brand new.

Life can be like the vacuum cleaner. We go along doing our every day-to-day routine, just like we always do, and everything seems just fine. Then one day comes a long, and though you may be doing the same routine, it doesn't feel like everything is fine. As a matter of fact, it seems that life has just hit a roadblock, and none of the routine seems to be working properly. The kids seem out of control, the spouse isn't listening to you any longer, the neighbors begin to irritate you, the job becomes completely boring, or it's so overwhelming that you can't think straight. The one thing in common with all these things is that none of them happened over night. They happen slowly. Something that I left out about the vacuum is that we figured it had been clogged for a while. How could that be? Simple, I wasn't paying attention to the cylinder filling up. It would take in some gradual dirt, but each time I vacuumed, it built up the clog even bigger, until the day came when nothing came through.

Is there something that you feel is blocked or stuck in your path? Is it that relationship that you long for? Is it your bank account and you just want it stay in the black until your next paycheck. Possibly it's the job, and you feel like you are at a dead end. Or even your relationship with God, asking yourself does He really hear my prayers? It may even be the fact that you are trying with all your might to get un-stuck, but nothing is happening. Jesus tells us in Matthew - "Come to Me all who are weary, and I will give you rest. Take My yoke upon you and learn from ME, for I am gentle and humble in heart, and you will find rest for your souls."

Today, whatever may be the "clog", I pray that our Sovereign Lord would give you clarity and rest, and that you will know where the "stuck place" is.

****

ASK YOURSELF:

What is God revealing to me today?

_____
_____
_____
_____
_____
_____

How do I see God working in my life today?

_____
_____
_____
_____
_____

What can I do to bring a blessing to someone else?

_____
_____
_____
_____

Journey Date 23 _____

At different times of the year, we can get a lot of rain. When we do I notice how incredible everything looks. Our rose bush has become a rose tree, standing over eight feet tall, the flowers have triple in size and the grass continues to grow faster than I can keep it cut. As I look at the beauty of the nature, I see a freshness and newness of the growth of things. I see new buds of life appearing in the flowers and on the trees. I see the clouds forming that bring down the rain. But the best part of the rain is the rainbow. After the rain falls and the sun shines the most beautiful sight is to see a rainbow.

Do you remember the last time you saw a rainbow and how you felt inside when you see one? The effect of "Wow" that overcomes you. Today I realized that "WOW" feeling is God revealing His promise one more time. He tells us in Genesis 9 "the rainbow is My reminder to Myself and to you that I have made a covenant with you, to never leave you, and that you are My creation."

You are HIS creation. He is delighted in you and sees His beauty in you.

Today He wants you to know that you are valuable to Him and He will stand in the covenant with you forever!

May the Lord rain down on you today with a ray of sunshine and a rainbow over your head.

****

ASK YOURSELF:

What is God revealing to me today?

_____
_____
_____
_____
_____
_____
_____
_____
_____
_____

How do I see God working in my life today?

_____
_____
_____
_____
_____
_____
_____
_____
_____
_____

What can I do to bring a blessing to someone else?

_____
_____
_____
_____
_____
_____
_____
_____
_____

Journey Date 24 _____

My husband and I took a trip to Colorado and stayed in a two-bedroom condo overlooking Dillon Lake. Bill invited his close friend, Ken and wife, Peggy, to join us for the week. We didn't really know Peggy very well (that's the wife of the friend). We have had dinner a few times, and gone to their house a few times, but nothing very lengthy. Plus, we have been gone from Houston for many years and people can change. It was going to be a trip that was of the unknown. I must admit that I was a little uncertain and anxious. Well, we were delightfully surprised with such a wonderful time. Ken and Peggy were so laid back and relaxed, it seemed as if we had known each other for a hundred years. By the end of the week, I felt so comfortable sitting around chatting or watching a movie. Peggy brought a sense of peace and comfort with her. Who knew that deep down inside Peggy and I would hit it off so good. (Well, she did take the trash out more than anyone else – kudos to her!)

Many years ago, a relationship started between me and God. In the beginning it was really good. As a matter of fact, you could say it was great. Then time passed by, and that relationship became a little unfamiliar. Not that God had changed over the years, but I certainly had. Then the day came when I realized that I wanted that comfortable feeling, that time of sitting and "chatting" with God. Deep down inside our relationship was really good, I just let it fall by the wayside. Paul writes this, *"... Praise to the Father of compassion and the God of all comfort, who comforts us in all our troubles, so that we can comfort those in any trouble with, the comfort we ourselves have received from God." 2 Corinthians 1:4*
Just like Peggy, God brings comfort, even in the worst or most difficult times.

Today, my prayer is that you can experience that comfort, whether you just meet Him today or if it has been 50 years ago. He longs to bring that blessing to you.

****

ASK YOURSELF:

What is God revealing to me today?

_____
_____
_____
_____
_____
_____
_____
_____
_____
_____

How do I see God working in my life today?

_____
_____
_____
_____
_____
_____
_____
_____

What can I do to bring a blessing to someone else?

_____
_____
_____
_____
_____
_____
_____
_____

I hear the rain falling. It is so long overdue. The ground is dry and cracked. The leaves on the bushes are wilty and some are even burned. The grass appears brown, brittle, and crusty, almost like its life is completely gone. Oh, how desperately we needed the rain. After a good long and hard rain, the foliage comes back to life. The trees and bushes no longer hang their leaves and branches low. The rain has filled their veins with water, which brings a freshness back to them. The dying grass perks up and each little blade appears happy, as if they were all standing up and dancing for joy. And the cracks that were so deep and dry are now filled with water. The water expands the dry ground, and the cracks begin to disappear and connect to each other to become solid whole ground again. Rain just seems to bring new life back from the dead and dying.

God tells us that He is the "living water", through Jesus Christ. This Living Water is different though.
Like the rain that falls on the dying grass and brings it back to life, so does the "Living Water". But, when we feel overwhelmed by life, or feel that life isn't worth living any longer, Jesus will pour Himself over us and refresh us with the Living Water. He fills us up with His love, and mercy and grace. Our "veins" get filled up with this "water" and feel alive again. There are a couple of differences in the rainwater and the Living Water...you have to ask for this Living Water. But, oh how much you receive when you do ask. Because you have asked, this water never lets you dry out completely again, this water gives you life forever! Let me write out what Jesus says in the book of John chapter 4 ...Jesus is talking to the Samaritan woman at the water well..."If you knew the gift of God and Who it is that asks you for a drink, you would have asked Him and He would have given you Living Water...."whoever drinks the water I give him will never thirst. Indeed, the water I give him will become in him a spring of water welling up to eternal life."

Today, if you have never experienced what it is to have the Living Water refresh you, I pray that you will be open to ask God for it. And, if you have received this Living Water, I pray that God would well up inside of you like a fresh spring and reveal to you His grace, mercy, and love all over again.

****

ASK YOURSELF:

What is God revealing to me today?

_____
_____
_____
_____
_____
_____
_____
_____
_____
_____

How do I see God working in my life today?

_____
_____
_____
_____
_____
_____
_____
_____
_____

What can I do to bring a blessing to someone else?

_____
_____
_____
_____
_____
_____
_____
_____

Journey Date 26 _____

I just love the Fall time of year, to walk outside and feel a cool wind blowing and smell a freshness in the air. Even though you can't see the wind, you know it's there because you can feel it. But, as time passes by, days, weeks, months and years, there will be circumstances that bring joy and sorrow, riches and losses, pain and healing, and other things that are seen and real, and yet time goes on. The one thing that is for sure, is that there will always be a wind that blows that we cannot see.

The wind is so mysterious. It is a creation that God made. The one thing that we cannot see, but we feel. Sometimes the wind is so strong and powerful, that it is difficult to walk or stand in it. Then sometimes, it gently moves and almost whispers in your ear.

I believe the wind is like our Lord. I know that I cannot reach out and physically touch Him, but I can feel Him and know His presence. Sometimes He speaks so loudly that I cannot ignore His presence. Then His gentle presence is known by people like you, by your love and your generosity. His Word tells us, "While our minds are not on the things which are seen, but on the things which are not seen; for the things which are seen are for a time; but the things which are not seen are eternal." 2 Cor. 4:18

Today "feel the wind" and remember that His Presence is always near you.

****

ASK YOURSELF:

What is God revealing to me today?

_____
_____
_____
_____
_____
_____
_____
_____
_____

How do I see God working in my life today?

_____
_____
_____
_____
_____
_____
_____
_____
_____

What can I do to bring a blessing to someone else?

_____
_____
_____
_____
_____
_____
_____
_____
_____

So, how many of you out there have ever written a love letter? That doesn't mean that you had to send it to anyone, but have you ever sat down and poured your love out on a piece of paper? My father showed me some letters that he and my mom shared before they were married. Things were really "swell" in their letters, but what I found most amazing was the date stamp on the letters. The first couple of letters were written about a week or so apart. Then the letters were 3 or 4 days apart. Then the postmarks were every day back and forth. At the last of the letters, I saw that each of them mailed letters on the same day. It was fun to read about their daily lives, missing each other, and longing to be together. But I kept looking at the postmarks… Jan 10, 1953; Jan 12, 1953; Jan 13, 1953, Jan 14, 1953…and they kept going. It was as if the letters had this urgency about them to get to the other persons hands. They carried such important information back and forth, they carried love back and forth, they carried the day-to-day life happenings back and forth. They were the connection between two people.

I imagine that people today probably don't write many love letters. Texting seems to be the thing to do… you know, "i luv u ☺", or "c u 2nite". Don't get me wrong, I think texts are fun, but there just seems to be something missing about the detail of the letter, and the postmark of the letter. To read these words say so much more, "I miss you, and feel alone without you. I can't wait to be close to you and share what is heavy on my heart. The distance that keeps us apart is difficult on most days."

As one of God's children we are so fortunate to have the most perfect love letter there is… the Bible. Some may say that the Bible are "just words" made up by man. I believe that all the words, are God breathed, they are such beautiful words and promises. Psalm 4:8 tells us to sleep peacefully… " *I will lie down and sleep in peace, for You alone, O Lord make me dwell in safety."* Psalm 139 tells us how much God knows us… *"Oh Lord you have searched me and You know me…You know when I sit and when I stand, You have Your hand upon me."* And in John 5:24, Jesus tells us that we can live forever – *"I tell you the truth, whoever hears My word and believes in Me, will have eternal life."*

God offers such a wonderful love letter, yet so many times we forget about it. We lose the urgency to have it in our hands, like the love letters that were sent between my parents. Oh, how God longs for our hearts to leap at the thought of reading one of His promises.

Today, if your heart longs for the passion of a love letter that you think is long-gone, pick-up God's word and read Song of Solomon, or the Psalms. You will see His amazing handwriting on the paper and note that the postmark has never changed but is always addressed to you.

****

ASK YOURSELF:

What is God revealing to me today?

_____
_____
_____
_____
_____
_____

How do I see God working in my life today?

_____
_____
_____
_____
_____
_____

What can I do to bring a blessing to someone else?

_____
_____
_____
_____
_____
_____

Have you ever made a promise to someone? I imagine if you are reading this, then the answer would be yes. There are all kinds of promises. Of course, the first one that I think of is my marriage vow or promise. I made a promise before God, friends, family and my husband that I would stay with him until "death do us part." Now I can tell you, there have been times that I thought that might happen and then my promise would be ended. (Obviously it is not God's plan for us to be apart yet.) But there are many other promises. What about a credit card, or a car note or a mortgage - you made a promise to that company that you would pay back the money that was borrowed. You signed your name on a dotted line and said, "Yes, I promise to pay you back what I owe you, plus interest." Or how about the many promises parents make to their children, especially when they are small. I remember my kids asking, "Mommy, can we go get ice-cream later if I help out around the house?"... My response .... "Sure honey, that's a great idea." Then later comes and goes and we never make it to the ice-cream store. Or the best one yet I would say to my kids, "I promise after school today we will go and _____ "(fill in the blank). And guess what, we never make it to the fill in the blank space.

Now as most promises are meant to be kept, and are said in good faith, sometimes they just get broken or are not kept. I imagine if you asked my children today how many promises did, I make and NOT keep, they could give you a long record of them. I hate to admit that on myself, but no point in trying to hide it - I think we have all fallen short of keeping a promise or two.

As I was thinking about this, my mind was flooded with many promises that God made to us. So many that I would be sitting here typing for probably 30 days and still not get them all listed. But there is one that has stuck out in my mind... Isaiah 49:15 & 16 ... "Can a woman forget her child, and not have compassion on her son? Surely, they may forget, Yet I will not forget you, See, I have inscribed you on the palms of My hands..."

Look down at your hands --- go ahead, look at them, can you imagine if those were God's hands - YOUR NAME is indelibly carved into those hands. That is HIS promise to you. Whenever He opens His palms, He sees your name written there. I imagine it is like a scar that will never go away because He doesn't want it to. What an incredible promise - one that will never be taken back or not fulfilled.

My beloved friend, let His hands reach out to you today and show you His love and your name that He has tattooed on His hands. Remember as you look at your hands, that the Father sees your name inscribed in His.
****

ASK YOURSELF:

What is God revealing to me today?

_____
_____
_____
_____
_____
_____

How do I see God working in my life today?

_____
_____
_____
_____
_____
_____

What can I do to bring a blessing to someone else?

_____
_____
_____
_____
_____
_____
_____

Water, what do you think of when you hear that word? Do you think of a lake, a pond, a swimming pool, boating, skiing, rain…water can be many things. It is probably the most sustaining drink around the world. Our bodies would not be able to function without water. It is a vital part of who we are. It is a vital part of all living creatures. A stray seedling made its way into a crack in the sidewalk next to our patio. The little seedling kept growing, even though I didn't give it any water. Through the dry hot days, it kept growing. It has grown to be over 3 feet tall now. But I wondered as slow growing as this tree is, how did this little guy get any water or nourishment to help it along? What was letting this little seed grow? How did the sunny days in the summer, no water, and no "real" ground to grow in, give nourishment to the tree. But there it was, getting taller and taller.

To my amazement I finally recognized that this little seedling is becoming an oak tree. An oak tree, hearty and strong, how was it surviving on nothing? Then just as I was staring at this little tree, Thomas, (one of the stray cats that I feed) walked up and rubbed along the little tree and moseyed on over to our water spigot and started licking it. As he sat there for several minutes, it dawned on me – the water faucet was leaking. The leak wasn't enough to notice, or make a difference in our water bill, but it was just enough to sustain the little tree. The dripping water fell to the ground and kept the roots wet, which kept the tree growing.

So many times, in our lives we are probably like that little tree. We try to stand when times are tough. We try to keep ourselves "watered" when we feel like we have been burned and are completely dry inside. I love how Isaiah writes the words from God, 58:11 – *The Lord will guide you always; He will satisfy your needs in a sun-scorched land and will strengthen your frame. You will be like a well-watered garden, like a spring whose waters never fail.* Isn't that wonderful news! Like the leaky faucet that kept dripping life into the ground for the little oak tree, our Sovereign God pours life into us, and gives us strength when we think we have none.

Are you thirsty today my friend, if so, just turn your eyes upon Jesus, and he will quench your thirsting heart.

****

ASK YOURSELF:

What is God revealing to me today?

_____
_____
_____
_____
_____
_____
_____
_____

How do I see God working in my life today?

_____
_____
_____
_____
_____
_____
_____
_____

What can I do to bring a blessing to someone else?

_____
_____
_____
_____
_____
_____
_____

Not long ago I took our cat, Samson, to the vet. He has a hard time breathing and makes a wheezing sound. If a cat snored, that's probably what it would sound like. As I was putting him in the cat carrier, he thought it was fun... at first. Then he realized I was locking the door and carrying him outside. He scrambled around in the carrier for a minute or so and then we took off in the truck. I could tell by his meowing and pacing back and forth in the carrier that he wasn't quite sure of what was going on. Each time he meowed; I would talk to him. I would speak in a soft voice and tell him "It's okay, we will be there soon". I would call out his name "Samson- sweet kitty - it's okay, I am here for you." He knew my voice which seemed to give him comfort for just the moments he could hear it, but then he would cry again. Our drive was about 10 minutes to the vet, but to him, it must have seemed like hours. When we arrived at our destination, I took him in the carrier and gave him to the veterinarian. He was checked over, got some medicine and we went back to the truck. I opened the cage and he calmly walked out and crawled in my lap. He knew he had to trust me to get him back home safely. I continued to talk to him and hold him close, and then opened the door of the carrier. Willingly he went back inside and laid down. It was as if he knew he had to trust me and not his own instincts.

Proverbs 3:5-6 Tells us to do same thing with our lives and God. "Trust in the Lord with ALL your heart and lean not on your own understanding, in ALL your ways acknowledge Him and He shall direct your paths." God knows what place you are in. He knows the "cat carrier" of your life and hears you calling out to Him. He knows the pains, the hurts, the heartaches, the trials. He knows the joy, the laughter, and the tears that you cry.

Today, even for just a moment, tell Him you trust Him with your life and your circumstances, and HE will take care of you.

****

ASK YOURSELF:

What is God revealing to me today?

_____
_____
_____
_____
_____
_____
_____
_____
_____

How do I see God working in my life today?

_____
_____
_____
_____
_____
_____
_____
_____
_____

What can I do to bring a blessing to someone else?

_____
_____
_____
_____
_____
_____
_____
_____
_____

I was on an adventure to find a cheese factory. This time though it was a little different, my loving, never say die, husband, was with me. Now, just like me, he used the internet to locate a cheese factory, and plugged the address into the Garmin. It was a different place in Wisconsin, but it sounded just as interesting as the first place I tried to find. There was one little difference though. This cheese factory required that you have NO jewelry on. Okay, if you know me, it is very difficult for me not to wear jewelry... especially my wedding ring. But my husband was adamant that we couldn't wear any jewelry. It didn't, make a whole lot of sense to me. I have been on many different tours, of all kinds of places, and never have I been asked to remove my jewelry. What in the world made this one so different?

We arrived at the factory (yep, we found it) and it was much a surprise to me, as this was an old fashion cheese factory. It was still run the same way that it was done over 80 years ago. This place still used the open vats to prepare the milk, and the labor was all manual. They were hand pouring the cheese curds into the molds, and they were using the original bricks to press the whey out of the cheese. They used special handmade tools to cut the cheese bricks. The cheese was hand dipped in salt brine, and then rolled into a warming room for it to age. After the entire process was completed and the cheese was ready to be packaged that was also done by manual labor. Nothing was processed or moved with machinery. Now it made sense why we couldn't wear jewelry. Can you imagine chomping into a big bite of 4-year-old cheddar only to find a silver shaped flower stud in your cheese? Not good! They were very protective of their processes. They wanted to make sure that no contaminates "fell" into their delicate cheeses.

Psalm 24: 4-6 tells us to do the same thing with our lives, as the cheese factory told us to do with our jewelry – " *Only the clean-handed, only the pure-hearted; Men who won't cheat, women who won't seduce. God is at their side; with God's help they make it.* (The Message) As humans it is difficult for us to always be clean...I am the first to admit that. But, like the family who owned the cheese factory who wanted their product to be the best, and not have chance for "foreign objects", God desires that of us as well. When we feel that there is a wall between us and Him, maybe He is just wanting us to "remove our jewelry" and talk to Him genuinely and honestly.

Today, I pray that you know that God wants you to be just who are with Him... jewelry or not.... He truly loves you!

****

ASK YOURSELF:

What is God revealing to me today?

_____
_____
_____
_____
_____
_____
_____

How do I see God working in my life today?

_____
_____
_____
_____
_____
_____
_____

What can I do to bring a blessing to someone else?

_____
_____
_____
_____
_____
_____
_____

Have you ever had something happen in your life that was so bizarre, that you thought you might have been on Candid Camera? Bill and I arrived home from a weekend trip to find what appeared to be a rock lying on the floor, next to our bed. At first, I thought that maybe one of the cats had one of those "cat moments", when the extra hair decided to make its way back out of their digestive system. With further investigation we discovered along with this rock object, there was broken glass all over the floor. We figured it out, a kid must have thrown that "rock" through the window. As we pulled the curtain back and opened the blinds, we were both stunned. There were two perfectly round 8" holes in our windows. We live in a mobile home, so there are two glass panes for each window. Both panes had holes in them. The strange part about these holes, beside the fact that they were perfectly round, is that they were higher up the window than I was tall, and the hole on the outside pane was about 2" above the hole on the inside pane. If a kid had thrown that rock, it should have been on the lower part of the window, and the glass would have probably shattered.

As we cleaned up the broken glass and debris, we noticed that the rock appeared to be broken in half. How in the world did half a rock create such perfectly round holes in the windows? We stood scratching our heads thinking that this half a rock had to have been a meteorite or asteroid. It was very puzzling. Finishing up the cleaning, I walked into the bathroom and lying on the rug in front of my sink was the other half of the rock. We are talking about 9 feet away, and around a corner, from where we found the first part of the rock. The pieces fit exactly. What was this thing? Where did it come from? Did a meteorite really fly through "our" bedroom window? What are the odds of this happening?

At first, I joked about it saying, "God must be wanting our attention because He is throwing things at us." The more that I thought about it though, God had to have directed that little piece of rock to go right where He wanted it. I believe He was wanting us to listen to Him, and to know that no matter what happens in our lives **HE** is still in control. He gives us a free will to hear to His voice and follow Him. Jesus tells us this in John 10:27-28 – *"My sheep listen* *to My voice; I know them, and they follow Me. I give them eternal life, and they shall never perish; no one can snatch them out of My hand."*

You may not have had a flying piece of rock come through your window, but you may be dealing with something else, like a death in the family, the loss of a job or the betrayal of a friend or significant person in your life. It could be that God has been trying to talk to you for some time, but life just keeps getting in the way. Sometimes the bizarre things aren't so bizarre, but they certainly do get our attention. When we follow the Lord though, He gives us the promise that we will have eternal life with Him and no matter what comes "flying into our lives", He will take care of us.

Today, my prayer is that we would all have better ears to hear the voice of the Lord and know that HE wants us near to Him.

****

ASK YOURSELF:

What is God revealing to me today?

_____
_____
_____
_____

How do I see God working in my life today?

_____
_____
_____
_____
_____

What can I do to bring a blessing to someone else?

_____
_____
_____
_____

Journey Date 33_____

I remember growing up and hearing the saying, "Absence makes the heart grow fonder." I wasn't too sure of what that meant until I got older. You know what that message really means, right?... "Leave now honey, because you are driving me crazy, and I need some time alone - but don't be gone too long, because I will miss you soon." In years past my husband traveled quite a bit. He would be gone two or three weeks at a time and then return for a weekend and then depart again. As a family, we began to get use to his schedule and "know" that he would return. But Charlie, our German Shepherd, wasn't always so sure of that. No matter if Bill was gone one day or one month, Charlie would ALWAYS great him with a hug and a smile that only a dog could give (literally the dog would get up on the bed and put his paws on Bills' shoulders and lay his head on on Bills' chest).I have thought about this saying lately and realized it is not a very good statement when you want a relationship to grow. I think time apart helps me to understand how much I desire to have a "daily" relationship with my husband, not just the weekends. Charlie didn't know any different, he just knew that he was to "love" on Bill every time Bill walked through the door.

We should be like Charlie with our relationship with God. God so desires for us to have that "daily' relationship with Him. He doesn't want to wait for weekends when "we" walk through "His" doors. He wants us to develop that relationship every single day and not wait to be absent from Him to have a closer relationship.

I hope today, no matter where you are with God, tell Him how much you love Him and let Him walk into the door of your heart.

****

ASK YOURSELF:

What is God revealing to me today?

_____
_____
_____
_____
_____
_____
_____
_____
_____

How do I see God working in my life today?

_____
_____
_____
_____
_____
_____
_____

What can I do to bring a blessing to someone else?

_____
_____
_____
_____
_____
_____
_____
_____

It was pitch black, driving down the highway, early a.m. The streetlights were off, and few cars were traveling on the road. Dividing stripes were the only thing I could see, as my headlights moved along the road. But it was a very familiar road, one that I had driven many times. Driving in the dark didn't bother me. In some strange way it was almost peaceful and comforting. There was a feeling of familiarity and complacency. Then, just as the drive had become routine, a very large, life size, black blob appeared in my sight. It had approached my vehicle very quickly, giving me a little fright. It was a person, hitch hiking. The hitch hiker was dressed in all black, only to see their similarity of a human shape. It seemed odd that this person was hitch hiking at 5:00 a.m., and then to be dressed in all black seemed a little odder. It was almost as if they really didn't want to be seen or noticed.

Our lives can be like this. Going along, everything seems "normal" and our life routines are mundane and complacent. Then "POW", something hits you. You didn't even know something was coming. Where did it come from? Why do you feel different? What happened? Has something been compromised? Has something shown up in your life that doesn't seem like it belongs? We have an enemy who prowls like a roaring lion, who sneaks up on his prey and then devours them. (1 Peter 5:8) Like the person hitch hiking, the enemy can seem like he is nowhere close, and then "it" happens. "It" appears in many forms, one too many drinks, one more phone call that shouldn't have happened, one more text message or email that "pushed the envelope", one more fight or argument, and then all that you know falls apart.

Please don't misunderstand what I am saying… it isn't the drink, or the phone call or the argument that causes pain, havoc, confusion, and chaos in our lives. It's that we didn't even realize "it" was just waiting outside our door. God is not the author of confusion but is the author of peace. He desires to bring harmony, not chaos. (1 Cor. 14:33).

Today, what is "it" that is causing you pain and chaos? Tell Him about "it" and let Him bring you peace and comfort.

****

ASK YOURSELF:

What is God revealing to me today?

_____
_____
_____
_____
_____
_____
_____
_____
_____

How do I see God working in my life today?

_____
_____
_____
_____
_____
_____
_____
_____
_____
_____

What can I do to bring a blessing to someone else?

_____
_____
_____
_____
_____
_____
_____
_____
_____

Over the past few months my mind seems to wonder more than it used to. Staying focused on one thing was never a problem. Reading a good book always kept me captivated. Watching an intriguing movie kept me on the edge of my seat. Listening to speakers at the quarterly meetings kept me informed. Hearing a great song on the radio lifted my spirits. But now it is not unusual when reading a captivating book or watching an intriguing movie, my mind will just wonder off and start thinking about something else, or someone else. It is very possible if you are reading this "today" that <u>you</u> have crossed my mind while watching a movie, reading a book, or sitting in a meeting. Even as I sit and type these words my mind still contemplates and wonders off thinking, "I wonder who will read this"? So, at times, having a wondering mind can be very frustrating (especially to my precious husband who loves me anyway).

But, on the other hand it can be a wonderful thing. Have you just had someone pop into your mind, and you wonder how are they doing? When my mind wonders about people, it gives me an opportunity to lift their name up in prayer. It may be a very simple prayer, "Lord, bless my friend today" or "Lord you know their pain today, give them comfort." God already knows what each of us are doing and going through. For me, it is hard to imagine that God truly knows every single cell of every single person walking on the face of the earth. God is so focused on us that He never wonders and never forgets us. Psalm 139 is a great summation of how well God knows us and will always know us. Let me paraphrased: *"Lord, You know when I sit and when I rise, I am an open book to You, even from a distance You know what I'm thinking....For you created my inmost being; you knit me together in my mother's womb...You know me inside and out, You know every bone in my body...Like an open book, You watched me grow from conception to birth; all the stages of my life were spread out before You."* Isn't that just like a wonderful Father, to know His children from the moment they are born.

Today, I hope you are comforted to know that our Almighty Father knows you so well, that He will never forget you. You are His beloved!
****

ASK YOURSELF:

What is God revealing to me today?

_____
_____
_____
_____
_____
_____
_____
_____
_____

How do I see God working in my life today?

_____
_____
_____
_____
_____
_____
_____
_____
_____

What can I do to bring a blessing to someone else?

_____
_____
_____
_____
_____
_____
_____
_____

Journey Date 36_____

Another anniversary day for me and my husband. How many of us get chocolate or something good on that day? My husband is so sweet, he knows that I am losing weight and doesn't want to "overdo" the chocolate, but he also knows how much I LOVE chocolate, so, he may give me a small box of the tasty morsels. It's just enough to give me the taste of the delicious nougats, but not too much to make me overindulge. Now my daughter on the other hand told me that she felt some celebrations are overrated. Her exact statement to me was, "you know, I don't know why people can't just show love to each other every day instead of waiting for one day of the year." What a true statement that is. How do we show each other the love that needs to be shared every single day?

Though my husband is thoughtful and remembers this day with a special card, some candy, and flowers, he goes beyond that. He will bring me flowers when I least expect it, or when I have had a tough week. He will take me out to dinner when I have had to work long hours, or just don't feel like cooking some night. He will call me up and say, "hey let's go the movies tonight and have a date night". (Yes, we still go on dates.) I am blessed to be married to a man who can think away from the dates on the calendar and thinks with his heart and soul.

That is what our God is to us. He doesn't show us His love only one day a year... He shows us His love, every day, every hour, every minute, every second. God loved us so much, that He gave us more than chocolate and flowers. He gave us the most precious gift... His Son... "For God so loved the world that He gave His one and only Son." – John 3:16. WOW! I just can't imagine giving up one of my children. I would rather sacrifice myself, before sacrificing one of my own. But look at those words again... don't just skim over them... HE LOVES THE WORLD! Everyone in the world! You, me, our neighbors, people we like and people we don't like. Isn't that something to think about? Who is it today that you feel you just can't love? Let God love them today. Let God love you today. It's HIS present to you, every single day of your life.
May you receive His blessings today, and every day to follow.

****

ASK YOURSELF:

What is God revealing to me today?

_____
_____
_____
_____
_____
_____
_____
_____
_____
_____

How do I see God working in my life today?

_____
_____
_____
_____
_____
_____
_____
_____

What can I do to bring a blessing to someone else?

_____
_____
_____
_____
_____
_____
_____
_____
_____

Have you ever made a loaf of bread from scratch? The ingredients used to make bread is simple… bread flour, water, milk or powdered milk, sugar, salt, and yeast. When our kids were younger (before Bread Machine days) we use to make bread as a family. We would mix the ingredients together, then cover the dough and let it rise. After a couple of hours, we would knead the dough and then cover it again and let it rise again. Then one more time we would knead the bread and then put it in the pan and let it rise in the pan, and then put it in the oven to rise some more and cook. Now what is amazing to me is that without any of these ingredients your bread won't come out like a loaf of bread, it may come out flat, or hard as rock. Of course, after the Bread Machine arrived on the market, my mother-in-law gave us one for Christmas. We made Peanut Butter Bread, Dill Bread, Garlic Basil Bread, Cheese Bread, Rye Bread, all kinds of bread. BUT a few times we left out the yeast. With a bread machine you didn't have to watch it to make sure the bread was rising, so it was easy to forget the yeast. Needless to say, the bread was pretty sad. It was a big blob of hard dough. It was a three-inch tall, 2 lb. Loaf of bread… yep, it was bad. Isn't it funny how something so small as the amount of yeast that goes into bread can make such a big difference? Our pastor said something that has stuck in my head… "a little leaven, leavens the whole loaf".

In life today we can be the "yeast" and add something special to someone's life. A smile, a kind word, a helping hand, a phone call, even possibly going out of your way to take someone out to dinner or take dinner to them, can all be ways that you add something to someone else. You may be thinking that you have too much going on in your own life, and that you don't think you can be "the yeast" today. Then possibly you are someone who needs "the yeast" added to your life. Don't be afraid to ask, but also remember that giving can help calm the hurting places, and you can be "the yeast".

Ecclesiastes 4:9 tells us "Two are better than one, because they have a good return for their work." Who can you be the yeast to today?

Today, God has called you to be "the yeast", to be a little leaven in someone's life. If someone comes to your mind as you read this,

pick up the phone and give them a call. They may just "knead" a
little leavening.

****

ASK YOURSELF:

What is God revealing to me today?

_____
_____
_____
_____
_____
_____
_____
_____
_____

How do I see God working in my life today?

_____
_____
_____
_____
_____
_____
_____
_____
_____

What can I do to bring a blessing to someone else?

_____
_____
_____
_____
_____
_____
_____
_____
_____

Journey Date 38_____

Frequently stop to get something to drink while traveling. Bill loves Starbucks (like I am sure many of you do). He usually gets a "Grande' mocha latte'" which I think is another name for large cup of hot coffee with whole milk that comes out foamy. Obviously, you can probably tell that I don't drink coffee. My Starbucks cup is usually filled with good ole' hot chocolate with lots of whip cream on top. My daughter likes to have her Starbucks cup filled with "decaf caramel macchiato" (not sure if I even spelled that right). Now if we aren't taking a Starbucks stop, we may take a Sonic stop or Wendy's stop or "fill-up" our thirsts with something from the local gas station after we have filled up the car. It could be an ice-cold root-beer, or a bottle of apple juice, or even just a plain bottle of water. We usually get something that we think will satisfy that thirst in us.

But I love what Jesus has to tell us about being thirsty.... "If anyone is thirsty, let him come to Me and drink. Whoever believes in Me, as the Scripture has said, streams of living water will flow from within him." – John 7:37-38

Read it again… that is such a wonderful gift to offer us. A never-ending drink. A drink that goes beyond any thirst we could ever have. HE alone will fill us with the "living water" that is unstoppable. Oh, what a gracious Savior we have. How much He loves us to offer us the best thirst-quenching drink we would want. Is your cup being filled with things that are not satisfying? Are you wondering where or how will your next cup be filled? Let our Jesus come and pour His living water into you.

Today take a leap of faith and let Jesus fill your cup with His living water.

****

ASK YOURSELF:

What is God revealing to me today?

_____
_____
_____
_____
_____
_____
_____
_____
_____

How do I see God working in my life today?

_____
_____
_____
_____
_____
_____
_____
_____

What can I do to bring a blessing to someone else?

_____
_____
_____
_____
_____
_____
_____
_____
_____

Journey Date 39_____

Have you ever had one of those days, or weeks, or even months when you just want to throw up your hands and say, "I give up!" It seems that everything and anything that can go wrong, does go wrong. You begin to wonder if there isn't a gray cloud that follows your every footstep? In the past few weeks, we have encountered a few of the "really, you've got to be kidding" moments. The fuel injector on our pickup truck needs to be replaced (I think that's what it is), our television set blew out last night (it's only 12 years old), and our master bathroom flooded…twice, with the second time happening while we were out of town, so our bedroom furniture is in the middle of the dining room. And to top it off, for two weeks you start a exercise program, eat healthy and gain 2 pounds! Can we say pour me. Well, that's what I was beginning to think, until…

My daughter and I ran into an old friend that we haven't seen in a few years. She had two sons, the same ages of my two daughters. It was nice to chit chat, and do the normal "so how have you been, it's been a long time since we've seen each other?" And the words came out of her mouth that left me speechless. "Did you know that my son died?" After the momentary shock, I responded with "No, I am so sorry to hear that? What happened if I could ask?" She calmly said "A drug overdose. He struggled with that demon for so long. He is finally at rest from it." My heart sank even more. But the amazing thing was while talking to my friend, there was an amazing presence of peace about her. She had the pain and questions of why, but at the same time she had the peace that passes our understanding, knowing that her son is walking where angels walk. She had rest in her heart as well. I knew that she leaned on the one true Savior to give her that rest. Jesus tells us in Matthew 11: 28-30 "Come to Me all you who are weary and burdened, and I will give you rest. Take My yoke upon you and learn from Me, for I am gentle and humble in heart, and you will find rest for your souls. For My yoke is easy and My burden is light."

My problems seem so small. The strange blessings out of problems are that while we are here on earth, we will see answers. We will get a remodeled bedroom and bathroom. We will replace the old TV. The truck will get a new fuel injector. And hopefully with consistency the body will become healthier. God seems to remind me that today is just that… and we need to live to fullest that we can… "today".

Today I pray for each of you who have lost loved ones, and that our Lord would cover you in His mercy and rest in the days to come.

****

ASK YOURSELF:

What is God revealing to me today?

_____
_____
_____
_____
_____
_____
_____

How do I see God working in my life today?

_____
_____
_____
_____
_____
_____
_____
_____

What can I do to bring a blessing to someone else?

_____
_____
_____
_____
_____
_____
_____
_____

Journey Date 40_____

One Saturday morning was crisp and cool. So, all of the windows came open in my house to let the fresh air blow through. While reading, I could hear a few birds chirping outside. Then quite clearly the "coo" of a morning dove began. It was a very distinct "calling" from this dove. He cooed and he cooed, and he cooed. Louder and louder his beckoning became. There was no stopping him either. The fellow was determined to find his mate. It was like a continued, long song he was singing so that his "love" could find him easily. It was soothing and steady and so beautiful. Then after a great length of time, of hearing this dove cooing for the one he loved, …it stopped. Why did he stop? Did he tire of singing for her? Was she too far away that she couldn't hear him? Did he go somewhere else to try and find her? Did she just decide to not listen? Or did she fly to him, where they both could rest together somewhere, sitting side by side?

Our Father is so much like His creation, the morning dove. He calls out our name. He beckons us loudly, and he beckons us softly. He continues to call out for us, just waiting for us to answer Him. He longs to sit with us, side by side. But I wonder, does He think, "When will they come to Me? Can they hear Me? My voice is calling loudly and gently to caress My child who is hurting and in pain. My voice is crying for the one who feels alone and abandoned. My voice is singing out to bring a reminder of joy in the times of heartache. My voice is bringing salvation to one who is wondering and lost. My voice is for the one I love…. My voice is for you."

Psalm 145:18-19 tells us that we can call on the Lord and He will hear us… "The Lord is near to all who call on Him, to all who call on Him in truth. He fulfills the desires of those who fear Him; He hears their cry and saves them." These are wonderful words when we think no one is listening, or that no one really cares. He cares. He is listening. He wants you to talk to Him. He wants to hear your voice. He wants to sit by your side.

Today, my prayer is that as God nudges your heart, that you let Him hear you, comfort you, and love you.

****

ASK YOURSELF:

What is God revealing to me today?

_____
_____
_____
_____
_____
_____
_____
_____
_____

How do I see God working in my life today?

_____
_____
_____
_____
_____
_____
_____
_____
_____

What can I do to bring a blessing to someone else?

_____
_____
_____
_____
_____
_____
_____
_____
_____

Journey Date 41_____

I was remembering a time when my son was little, and he wanted a peanut butter and jelly sandwich. And of course, a good mom wouldn't deprive her children of such a want, so I made it for him. Now, we did have a rule in the house that you could only eat the table. No carrying food around the house. You can imagine, a four-year-old carrying a PBJ sandwich around the house, right?! Then a few days later, I was laying down in my bed, with my son to get him to take his nap, then a waft of the peanut butter aroma crossed my nostrils. I thought for a moment... I knew I didn't give him peanut butter that day, where could the peanut butter smell be coming from? The headboard on my bed had "secret hiding places". There were sliding doors with little cubby holes to put nick knacks and books in. I kept mine empty, or at least I thought they were. That flailing smell of the peanut butter was really beginning to intrigue me... I had to find out where it was coming from. Yep, you guessed it, hidden in the "secret place". As I slid the door open on the headboard, there was the PBJ from days ago. My son was nice enough to leave it on the plate, but it had become hard and crusty, and the bread was shriveling up to uncover the peanut butter and jelly.

I am not sure why I didn't get a whiff of the peanut butter smell before then, but God reminded me that unforgiveness is kind of like this sandwich. You see, if you hurt someone or someone hurts you, and forgiveness is not sought as soon as possible, then you can become hard and crusty, and begin to shrivel up on the inside and the outside. I know that there are some places in our lives that are difficult to ask for forgiveness and possibly harder places in our lives that we need to forgive... but I urge you today, to seek God and let Him show you if there are any "secret places" that need to be forgiven. When we don't forgive others or forgive ourselves it will hinder our relationship with God.

Jesus said, "For if you forgive men when they sin against you, your Heavenly Father will also forgive you. But if you do not forgive men their sins, your Father will not forgive your sins." - Matthew 6: 9-14

Today, don't let the peanut butter and jelly in your life stay hidden and bring an un-wanting aroma.

****

ASK YOURSELF:

What is God revealing to me today?

_____
_____
_____
_____
_____
_____
_____
_____
_____

How do I see God working in my life today?

_____
_____
_____
_____
_____
_____
_____
_____
_____

What can I do to bring a blessing to someone else?

_____
_____
_____
_____
_____
_____
_____
_____
_____

Journey Date 42_____

I was traveling and came home to find that, Samson, my cat, wasn't there. Apparently, he decided to sneak out while carpenters were coming in and out of the house. The problem is that even though Samson weighs in at 21.2 pounds, he is the biggest "chicken" cat there ever was. Plus, he is my son's cat, but since William moved out, Samson stayed behind and has adopted me as his "overseer". So, our relationship (mine and Samson's) is unique. Through this, I've realized that Samson was my connection to my son. Samson brings comfort to me in those nights when Bill is traveling. He purrs so loud that his whole body vibrates. And when he lays on my pillow, next to my head, the pillow vibrates. SO, I had to be proactive and try and find Samson. The creativity kicked in and "Missing Cat" flyers were made, and out to the streets I went.

Walking the streets and personally handing out flyers seemed to be the best way to go. My thoughts were that if Samson caught a glimpse of me, maybe he would come running. My neighbors were receptive and said they would keep an eye out for him. One neighbor said, "Oh, I saw that big yellow cat, he was trying to chase the rabbits." So, I walked, and I called out Samson's name, and I talked to God, and I walked, and I talked to God some more, and I cried, and I called out his name, and I walked some more, and cried some more.... I wondered, did God really know how much my heart was aching? He had to have known where Samson was, and God had to have known how much Samson meant to me. Why wouldn't God let Samson just walk right in front of me so that I could pick him up, squeeze him tight, and go home and all would be great? But that didn't happen, and the streets seemed to become abandoned. Where did everyone go? Don't they know how important to me it was to personally hand out these flyers and express my deepest pain at the moment?

Well, after 2+ days of Samson missing, and several hours that night wondering the streets and calling out Samson's name, he finally came home. Bill and I were outside moving some things from the truck into the house, and we could hear a very faint "meow". We dropped everything, and I called his name, and his teeny, little meow was like a sweet song to my ears.

It seems all so silly now, it's just a cat, right? He is just a cat, but he is important to me. While walking and calling out his name, and having tears fall in between, it seemed as if God was truly walking right next to me. Almost like a little nudge that said, "so, if you love your cat this much, how much more do you think that I love My children? My children are created by Me, and my heart aches when they go out and get lost. I call out their name, but they don't come running. I patiently wait, and continually call, but nothing, they are still wondering. Some are chasing things that they think will bring them happiness and joy, but I Am, the joy that they are seeking. I WILL keep calling, I just wish they would hear My voice and come home."

Do you feel lost and wondering around? Have you tried so many things that nothing seems to make sense, and no one has the answers? Have you lost hope in yourself or in the world? My heart takes me back to the wise words that our Savior spoke. John 3:16 – "For God so loved the world that He gave His only son, that whoever believes in Him shall not perish, but have eternal life." Each of us has the opportunity to spend eternity in God's home and never be lost again. He wants all His children by His side. He longs to give His joy to those who seek Him.

Today call out to Him, He has been calling out to you.
****

ASK YOURSELF:

What is God revealing to me today?

_____

_____

How do I see God working in my life today?

_____

_____

What can I do to bring a blessing to someone else?

_____

_____

Journey Date 43_____

Remember the story about Samson getting out of the house and getting lost, well he did it again. Samson has a way of greeting of us every evening after work, and when I came in the door and didn't get Samson's "happy dance" (as we call it), my heart sank. The first thought through my mind was that he got out again. Bill was in and out that day and he said he hadn't seen him most of the day. This time I wasn't going to panic. He did come home the first time, so he had to come home this time. Samson really didn't like "his home" and "his space" being messed with. If he could talk, he probably would have told us to leave everything just like it was and not to bring strangers in the house. Nighttime was approaching, the carpenters left, and I started to wonder, will Samson come home tonight? We sat down to watch a little television, and Bill could see the look on my face. Calmly he said, "Don't worry about Samson, he knows he has a good home, and he knows who feeds him. He will come home." Bill was right, and certainly worrying about Samson wouldn't benefit anyone. So, we sat relaxed, watching Deadliest Catch, and then we hear a very strange noise in the kitchen. Bill turned the television down and we heard it again. It sounded like glasses or dishes knocking against each other. It was a little strange, okay a lot strange. Bill got up and walked in the kitchen to see what the noise was. Just as he came around the corner in front of the kitchen cabinets, the bottom cabinet door opens, and out comes Samson. Now, I have no idea where in the world he was hiding, because there isn't any space in my kitchen cabinets, but apparently Samson didn't care. He wanted to be as far tucked away from the noise of the carpenters, and the fear of being outside again.

We laughed with relief that Samson was not outside, but it made me think. He went to great lengths to find a hiding place where he felt safe and secure. How many times have I longed for that place but was too afraid to search for it. It was those times when my heart ached, when finances were doubtful, when relationships seemed unrepairable, when my body was completely worn out, or when death streamed through my family. There was a longing deep inside for safe, secure, and quiet peace… Our God wants to give us that safe and secure place. Psalm 27:5 says it like this – "For in the day of trouble He will keep me safe in His dwelling: He will hide me in the shelter of His tabernacle and set me high upon a rock." (NIV) Let me write it out as the Message shows, "That's the only quiet, secure place in a noisy world. The perfect getaway far from the buzz of traffic."

You see, God has the perfect getaway for you and for me. It is in HIS tabernacle, in His presence, sheltered under His outstretched arms. We must ask Him for that security, and in the midst of the "noises of life", He will surely bring you the peace, the calm, the security and the quiet.

Today, tell Him that you want to sit by His side and that you want His loving arms wrapped around you.

****

ASK YOURSELF:

What is God revealing to me today?

_____
_____
_____
_____
_____

How do I see God working in my life today?

_____
_____
_____
_____
_____

What can I do to bring a blessing to someone else?

_____
_____
_____
_____
_____

Journey Date 44_____

While driving down the street, I was suddenly stopped by screaming sirens. A fire engine and ambulance pulled out of their station and onto to the road in front of me. I watched as they drove by and wondered where they were going. Just as quickly as I wondered, I saw the accident, just a few yards in front of me. The fire engine parked in the middle of the road to stop oncoming traffic to protect the vehicles involved - and the ambulance parked a few feet from the fire engine, closer to where the people, who were involved in the accident. I watched the firemen and emergency medical technicians go to work quickly on the scene. They went right to the problem to help and rescue the people who were in need. They stopped other vehicles from driving through the accident so that no more harm could happen.

I thought for a moment and realized that God is the same way with us. He runs to our rescue in our greatest times of need. He stops everything around us to get close to us. He waits to hear us call out to Him. He brings us His presence to give us comfort.

When you are in a time of need and you feel like you need to be rescued, remember Psalm 61: "Hear my cry O God, attend to my prayer. From the end of the earth, I will cry to You. When my heart is overwhelmed lead me to You, the Rock, that is higher than I. - Rescue me."

Today, do you need to be rescued? Call out His name, He is there to save you.

****

ASK YOURSELF:

What is God revealing to me today?

_____
_____
_____
_____
_____
_____
_____
_____
_____

How do I see God working in my life today?

_____
_____
_____
_____
_____
_____
_____
_____
_____
_____

What can I do to bring a blessing to someone else?

_____
_____
_____
_____
_____
_____
_____
_____
_____
_____

Journey Date 45_____

Hot, hot, hot and hotter! If you haven't guessed yet I am talking about the temperature here in Texas. A few years ago, when we had the 30 days of over 100 degrees, we couldn't keep up with watering the grass. It seemed as soon as we watered it, it dried up. It was a losing battle, and the heat was winning. So, we decided not to water the lawn. What could happen, except that the grass dies out until the next good rain, right? Not exactly, after a couple of weeks of not watering the lawn, we saw how brown it was getting. What we didn't expect to see was a patch of grass that was black. With closer inspection we found a cigarette butt lying in the center of the black patch of burnt grass. Our grass was actually on fire! We don't know if a neighbor saw it and put it out, or if by God's grace He snuffed it out, but we were very thankful it was out. From that hot summer to now, we water the lawn 2 or 3 times a day if it needs it. Of course, the lawn is now green and not brittle. We were determined never to be the situation of burnt grass again.

Our spiritual lives are much like that grass. When we stop "watering the spirit", our lives seem to "dry up" and get "burned out". We have all been in that place. Maybe you are there now. It's easy to get frustrated with life and just stop "watering" the good things in life. When we stop looking for the good in our lives, and we stop seeking answers from God, the "dried up" places seem to burn out of control. Isaiah tells us that all we have to do is ask God for the "living water" and the burnt places will be quenched. Let me write it out; 58:11 – *"The Lord will guide you always. He will satisfy your needs in a sun-scorched land and will strengthen your frame. You will be like a well-watered garden, like a spring whose waters never fail."*

Today, if you are in that burned out place, let someone know, or sit in a quiet place and let God know, He wants to strengthen you in this dry and barren times.

****

ASK YOURSELF:

What is God revealing to me today?

_____
_____
_____
_____
_____
_____
_____
_____
_____

How do I see God working in my life today?

_____
_____
_____
_____
_____
_____
_____
_____
_____
_____

What can I do to bring a blessing to someone else?

_____
_____
_____
_____
_____
_____
_____
_____
_____
_____

Journey Date 46_____

My daughter has told me over and over how important it is to wear sunglasses. She has shared with me how they protect the retina and help keep cataracts from forming. With the eyesight dwindling, regular sunglasses won't work. She convinced me to take the plunge and purchase prescription sunglasses. I wasn't too sure if I would really like them, but to help protect my eyes, it was worth taking the chance. The sunglasses came in, and they are wonderful. They are almost too wonderful. The glasses are so comfortable and lightweight, and they block out the sun so well. You wouldn't think that would be a problem, except when you forget to take them off, after you've gone inside a building. A couple of weeks ago, I walked into the house, sporting my new sunglasses on my face, and I couldn't figure out why everything seemed so dark and dreary. I turned on a couple of lights, but that didn't help much. I opened the blinds, and that didn't work either. I just kept thinking, wow, either my eyesight has gotten bad, or my house needed some new bright lights and paint. Continuing to walk toward my bedroom, I looked in a mirror, and sitting perfectly on my face… yep, were my sunglasses. Okay, don't laugh too hard, I bet I am not the only person who has done that. Okay, maybe so, but it was great revelation to me. Immediately the sunglasses came off and the regular glasses came on, and wah-la… everything was bright and beautiful.

Our lives can be like the sunglasses. You are going along fine, everything seems to be great, or at least you think it is, then the dark and dreary situations creep in. Sometimes it is the subtle things that take us down that path. The "boring job", the "annoying spouse", the "know it all co-worker", or the "angry child". It could be a situation that seems hopeless and feels like the sunglasses will never come off. Possibly the loss of a loved one, or the loss of a job. Maybe a friendship that you knew would never end, did. Or maybe abuse from a partner or family member. All these things can appear to be forever dark, but God tells us to look at life in a different way. 2 Cor. 4:16-18 – " *So we're not giving up. How could we! Even though on the outside it often looks like things are falling apart on us, on the inside, where God is making new life, not a day goes by without His unfolding grace. These hard times are small potatoes compared to the coming good times, the lavish celebration prepared for us. There's far more here than meets the eye. The things we see now are here today, gone tomorrow.* But, the things we can't see now, will last forever." (The Message Bible)

What a wonderful promise we have been given. Our eyes don't see what He has in store for us, but our heart and soul know deep down inside that something wonderful is coming.

Today, do not be discouraged, but know that a better place is coming for those who believe in Christ Jesus. "Our Glory land is just over yonder."

****

ASK YOURSELF:

What is God revealing to me today?

_____
_____
_____
_____
_____
_____

How do I see God working in my life today?

_____
_____
_____
_____
_____

What can I do to bring a blessing to someone else?

_____
_____
_____
_____
_____
_____

Journey Date 47_____

Wow, what a weekend. As many of you know my son, William, left for his first deployment on Sunday. On Saturday, the city of Denton gave a great celebration for the soldiers. (Kudos to you Denton!) A ceremony was held, the Brigadier General from Texas spoke and gave an awesome token for the Unit to take to Afghanistan, honor was shown, people clapped, and prayers were prayed. Yep, they actually got permission to pray in Jesus name, and the rest of the day the soldiers were able to spend with their families. Then Sunday came. 6:30 am, we received a text message from William, "come soon". We weren't sure we were going to be able to see him Sunday, but we did and were so blessed. The soldiers were all in line, "weighing in", hoping that their bag and their body weighed under 350 pounds. Patiently we waited, as they did. When the last soldier was through the line, we expected them to start loading up shortly. A couple of hours went by, then another, and another, and another. Only to find out that one of the buses had not made it to transport the soldiers to the airfield. We were able to spend 7 more precious hours with our son. Some moments were still and quiet, some were full of laughter, some were solemn and tearful. But all of them are moments that each of us will cherish until he comes home.

Then the time came for their formation. "ooo-rah" I think I heard someone yell and all of the soldiers came quickly and lined up. They were ready. They were prepared. They accepted a call on their lives that only a select group will do. Orders were yelled out, and a few tears were even shed by the soldiers, and then they left to load onto the buses. Watching them, willingly, knowingly, fearlessly board those buses must be one of the most difficult things, and yet one of the proudest things that a parent could feel. William made the choice to serve his country… but oh, as a parent, how my heart hurt, and the tears fell, and continue to fall now. The ache inside of me is not describable, but I am sure there are many of you who know exactly what that feeling is.

Monday morning came and the heartache was still so real. I sobbed heavy tears and cried out to God, and it hit me… God knew exactly how I felt. He watched his Son come to a broken earth, willingly, knowingly that He would give up His life for us. How did God do it? How did He sit and watch His son lovingly and courageously give Himself up? But God did. And because He did, we have been given a chance to live life forever in Heaven, and to have grace and mercy while we are here on earth. "For

God so loved the world that He gave His one and only Son, that whoever believes in Him will not perish, but have life everlasting!" ~John 3:16

Today, I know that my son and his comrades, and the many soldiers before and after him, are serving as they felt called to do. I also know that we have been given the greatest gift, God's Son, Jesus Christ because He was called to do so. Don't take Him for granted but give Him thanks today. And when you see an American Soldier, tell him thank you too.
****

ASK YOURSELF:

What is God revealing to me today?

_____
_____
_____
_____
_____
_____
_____

How do I see God working in my life today?

_____
_____
_____
_____
_____
_____
_____

What can I do to bring a blessing to someone else?

_____
_____
_____
_____
_____
_____
_____
_____

Journey Date 48_____

Okay, I must tell you a story about a friend. I hope they don't mind me sharing this story, but it is too good not to share. About a month ago my friend received her new Droid X2 and was thrilled. She was so excited because of the great things that she had heard about the camera function on the phone. The reason she was excited is because she is a photographer by profession. She took her first pictures with enthusiasm only to see that they weren't so good. Nothing came out clear and most came out with a "foggy" look. So, she took more pictures… same thing… foggy, out of focus, and unclear. Getting a little frustrated because the phone wasn't living up to the standards that she heard about, she decided to take a few more pictures. Still not good. I have a feeling by this time she was either ready to throw the phone at someone or give Verizon a major "what for" because the phone just wasn't living up to the expectations she had. So today, she was taking pictures of that "silver lined cloud" while driving home and saw that it had that little sticky plastic thing over the camera lens. You know those pieces of plastic that are on microwaves, new watches, or most anything that has a glass lens or cover. Of course, after she took the plastic cover off the lens, the photos were awesome, just like she expected.

When I read her story on FB (I figure since it's there, it is okay to write about) it made me think about how many times we see through a "foggy" lens. Situations can look different because the mind is not thinking clear. We try and try to make a situation "fit" only to continue to have failure and frustration occur. It is difficult to take a step back and re-think what is happening, especially when we are comfortable where we are at. We can even be comfortable in the bad and unhealthy situations because we are afraid to take off the "sticky plastic thing" and see the beautiful truth. In John 8, Jesus tells us - "If you hold to My teaching, you are really My disciples. Then you will KNOW the truth, and the truth WILL set you free." It is the recognition of truth, by personal experience, that allows us to be free from the fog and walk in clarity.

Today, take a moment to evaluate the truth in your life. We have an opportunity to recognize and understand what truth is and to be free indeed.

****

ASK YOURSELF:

What is God revealing to me today?

_____
_____
_____
_____
_____
_____
_____
_____
_____

How do I see God working in my life today?

_____
_____
_____
_____
_____
_____
_____
_____
_____
_____

What can I do to bring a blessing to someone else?

_____
_____
_____
_____
_____
_____
_____
_____
_____

Journey Date 49_____

Life is an interesting word. Today it seems that the word "life" means "to hurry". How many times in a day do you hurry to get all your chores done? How many times do you tell your children or your co-workers that we need to "hurry up and get this done because we have so many other things to do". How many meetings, soccer games, rehearsals, and deadlines do we all have on our platter each day? And some days the platter seems like it is so full that we just want to stop and yell "NO MORE!" Even when we think we are accomplishing the things that need to be done, and start peeling the pieces off the platter, more gets added and the platter seems too never be empty. Then the toppings on the platter is piled with stress, then a little anxiety is poured on, and then worry and depression may become the final topping.

David tells us in the Psalms that we need to be still and know that God is our refuge and strength. "God is our refuge and strength, an ever-present help in trouble. Therefore, we will not fear..." Psalms 46:1. God tells us in Psalm 46:10 - "Be STILL and know that I AM GOD!"

I hope today as your "life" continues to bring new challenges that you will take the time to stop and just be still. Turn off the TV, turn off the radio, and if you can, go into your closet and just rest in Him and be still and know that HE is God. HE is your refuge.

****

ASK YOURSELF:

What is God revealing to me today?

_____
_____
_____
_____
_____
_____
_____
_____
_____
_____

How do I see God working in my life today?

_____
_____
_____
_____
_____
_____
_____
_____
_____

What can I do to bring a blessing to someone else?

_____
_____
_____
_____
_____
_____
_____
_____
_____

Journey Date 50_____

I had to mail a letter this week, so I stuffed everything in the envelope and then as most of us do, I licked the flap and sealed the envelope. I wrote my return address on the outside of the envelope, stuck the stamp on it, was just about to take it to the mailbox and remembered…. "Oh no, I forgot to put something in there!" By now the "glue" on the seal was stuck! No un-sealing it. I gently pulled on the envelope, trying not to tear it. No luck, I couldn't get the envelope opened. I wasn't at home, so I couldn't try the "steam thing" on it. So, I don't know if that really works. What was I going to do? I wanted to put something else in the envelope, but there was no way. The only thing that was a guarantee was that the letter that I sealed was going to get mailed, just like it was.

Did you know that God does the same kind of thing with us? Let me show you how I know…

Ephesians 1:13 and 14- "In Him you also trusted after you heard the word of truth, the gospel of your salvation; in whom also, having believed, you were sealed with the Holy Spirit of promise, who is the guarantee of our inheritance until the redemption of the purchased possession to the praise of HIS glory."

Isn't that something – He "seals" us with Himself, the Holy Spirit, and we are guaranteed to live in His kingdom forever. All we have to put in our "envelope" is the word of truth, and our salvation and it is a guarantee that we are "sealed" and no one can "un-seal" us. Not even ourselves. Circumstances may seem difficult and hopeless and look like the "seal" has been broken and "other things" are trying to be "stuffed" into the envelope… but this is God's promise… WE ARE SEALED!!!

I pray today that God would fill you with an abundance of His Holy Spirit, to guide you, to hold you, to give you hope but most of all to show you how much you are loved.

****

ASK YOURSELF:

What is God revealing to me today?

_____
_____
_____
_____
_____
_____
_____
_____
_____

How do I see God working in my life today?

_____
_____
_____
_____
_____
_____
_____
_____
_____
_____

What can I do to bring a blessing to someone else?

_____
_____
_____
_____
_____
_____
_____
_____
_____
_____

Journey Date 51_____

When the company that I work for built their building, they left a small piece of heavily wooded land to the south of the building. Someone decided that a walking trail should be cut through the heavy woods, along with a sitting area in the middle of the woods. There are large granite benches to sit on and a gravel and dirt pathway wind its way up and down the hilly grounds. I'm not sure how long the trail is, but I've heard it's about one-quarter of mile long. Recently, with the cooler temperatures, it seemed like the perfect place to spend lunchtime. So that's where my feet took me. Once, twice, three, four, five times around the trail. Not being in the best of shape, my feet decided they needed a rest on the benches. The shadows of the trees overtook the sitting area. There was hardly any light to see through the thick woods. It isn't nighttime, so you can still see through the trail, but it was interesting to notice that everything in that little wooded area seemed to be so isolated. I knew there was a big building to the right of me, and that the freeway was just ½ mile in front of me. And only yards away was the main street that brought people to our building. But right there, in that very space, it was quiet and still. How nice it was to just stop. I thought about my children, and my husband. I thought about my father and my stepmother and their decisions for the future. I thought about the people that I work with every day, and I probably thought about you, as one of the many blessings in my life.

While sitting there, my heart wanted to know that Christ was the leading light in my life (to the best of my ability), and that He would keep His light upon ALL His children, no matter where they were at, or what "wooded" place they may be in. Just as my thoughts and prayers came, so did an amazing ray of Light. Right through the heavily wooded forest, an opening to the sky appeared and a strong, warm, bright, ray of Light beamed down. It was as if Christ Himself said, "here I am, here I will be, here will I go, I will always be by your side and by the side of those that you love." It was wonderful to know that He is taking care of "my" beloved friends and family. Jesus tells us – "I have come as a Light into the world, that whoever believes in Me should not abide in darkness." – John 12:46. How comforting to me, to know, that Christ is our Light and our guide, even when we don't think He is there, He is.

Today, my prayer is that you could find a quiet place, even for just 5 minutes, and that you would allow the Lord Jesus pour out His warm, bright Light upon you.

****

ASK YOURSELF:

What is God revealing to me today?

_____
_____
_____
_____
_____
_____
_____
_____
_____

How do I see God working in my life today?

_____
_____
_____
_____
_____
_____
_____
_____
_____

What can I do to bring a blessing to someone else?

_____
_____
_____
_____
_____
_____

Journey Date 52_____

This past weekend I was in Chicago with my husband and daughter. One afternoon I went outside to feel the crisp air. The wind was blowing slightly, and the temperature was around 55 degrees. It was just about as perfect as it could be, especially coming from warm Texas. Occasionally a strong wind would blow thru, and I could hear something like a group of people applauding. I looked around trying to figure out where that sound was coming from. Then it would go away. Sure enough a strong wind would blow through and there was the sound again. As if hundreds of people were clapping their hands together. I looked again – couldn't see anything. Finally, I asked, "Lord, where in the world was this sound coming from?" Suddenly, the wind blew stronger again, and the clapping was strong and loud and continuous. So, I turned quickly to look behind me and aha! – there it was, two 30 foot plus, tall Maple trees, clapping their leaves together. The stronger the wind blew, the louder the clapping was. It truly sounded like hundreds of people clapping.

Now the strange thing about this, is that when I first went outside, I was talking with God, I was asking some direct questions to God. Questions that I needed to know if I was heading in the right direction. There HE was, once again, in the wind, clapping, applauding, saying "yes" go that way. Every time I asked a risky question, He always answered with an applause of the clapping of the leaves.

Applause or clapping is such an outward show of how we feel. When we clap our hands we show our approval, our appreciation, our love, and our excitement. I love to worship God, Jesus, and the Holy Spirit with singing, clapping and raising of my hands. I know HE loves for us to worship Him. God was doing the same to me on this Saturday afternoon. He wasn't worshiping me, but He was applauding me for asking Him for direction. I found a verse in Isaiah that blew me away – God tells us, "For you shall go out with joy, and be led out with peace; The mountains and the hills shall break forth in singing before you, and all the trees of the field shall CLAP THEIR HANDS" – Isaiah55:12

Isn't that something, He already wrote about His trees clapping for us. "WOW! – Thank you, Lord, for loving us so much!"

I pray today that you can hear God's applause. Sit out on your patio, and just listen to Him. He is there.

****

ASK YOURSELF:

What is God revealing to me today?

_____
_____
_____
_____
_____
_____
_____
_____

How do I see God working in my life today?

_____
_____
_____
_____
_____
_____
_____
_____
_____

What can I do to bring a blessing to someone else?

_____
_____
_____
_____
_____
_____
_____

Journey Date 53_____

While driving through my neighborhood, I noticed the number of American flags that were waving in the wind. One of my neighbors has a spotlight that shines from the ground up to the flag. In the deep and darkness of the night that flag stands out above everything on the street.

As I saw this flag flying and moving so gently in the wind, I thought about how free it looked. Nothing holding it down, nothing stopping it from swaying back and forth. Freedom is an awesome thing. If you had to describe freedom to someone, how would you describe it? I think of the freedom I have been given to choose where I live, who I married, how many children I could have and what I could name my children. I think of the many soldiers who put their lives on the line, fighting for freedom and standing for justice. But most of all, I think of the freedom to love the Lord my God with all of my heart, with all of my soul and all of my mind. You see it is a choice that God gives us. He gives the freedom to speak boldly about Him, to help others in need, to release us from our dark places by trusting in Him. Just like the flag that waves in the darkness, that is who HE is to us. He stands out above the rest of the world and His Spirit moves to and fro and gives us freedom.

"The Spirit of the Sovereign Lord is on me, because the Lord has anointed me to preach good news to the poor. He has sent me to bind up the brokenhearted, to proclaim FREEDOM for the captives and release them from the darkness to proclaim the year of the Lord's favor..." Isaiah 61: 1 & 2

I hope today that if you have any captive places, that you let Him set you free. Let His Spirit move to and fro in you and feel His freedom to heal any broken places in your heart.

Know today that someone, somewhere is praying for you

****

ASK YOURSELF:

What is God revealing to me today?

_____
_____
_____
_____
_____
_____
_____
_____
_____

How do I see God working in my life today?

_____
_____
_____
_____
_____
_____
_____
_____
_____

What can I do to bring a blessing to someone else?

_____
_____
_____
_____
_____
_____
_____
_____
_____

As most of you may know, my husband and I feed a couple of stray cats in the neighborhood. We have named them, for the sake of being able to identify which cat is who. Stripes (the tabby stripped one) and Thomas (the big Tom cat) have gotten us figured out. When they hear us open the door, they come running from wherever they are at. They know where to go to get a free meal. Even when my kids come over, it's as if the cats know what kind of cars they drive, especially Thomas. He comes up the car door and waits for Betty or Katy to walk up to the house. Thomas knows that if Bill or I don't feed him, then one of the girls will feed him. They really are smart. They have no place to call home. They wander all over the neighborhood. They don't have a nice warm and cozy place to lay at night. BUT we do have Samson and Chicago Girl, our indoor cats. They too get "fed" well and treated good. Funny thing though, they don't come running when we put food down in their bowl. They may saunter in and sniff the food, maybe take a bite or two, then saunter away with the attitude of "I will eat when I want too".

It's interesting that the cats with no home, and no structure, living moment to moment, know where to run to for food. And the cats that live in a warm and loving home really treat us like we owe them something.

In some ways I think we as humans can be that way with our Lord. How many of us know someone who has been struggling, financially, emotionally, physically, or possibly homeless, and they run to the Lord because they know He will take care of them. Then there are those of us who have just about anything we need or want, and we can take care of ourselves. To rely on someone else, or even God for help is not "necessary". We don't need someone to "feed" us because we can do it on our own. It's not that God doesn't want us to be responsible, because I believe He does. However, He does want to have a relationship with us, even in those times that we feel we don't need Him as much.

Today, whether you are a person in "need", or not, know how much God loves to take care of you in the good times and the bad.

****

ASK YOURSELF:

What is God revealing to me today?

_____
_____
_____
_____
_____
_____
_____
_____
_____

How do I see God working in my life today?

_____
_____
_____
_____
_____
_____
_____
_____
_____

What can I do to bring a blessing to someone else?

_____
_____
_____
_____
_____
_____
_____
_____
_____

Journey Date 55_____

Many of you have heard me talk about my German Shepherd, Charlie, and the many things that I learned from him. Well Charlie is no longer with us. For several months he began having problems walking, and then more problems with his bladder. We took him to the vet to have him checked out, only to find that he had over 20 bladder stones and acute arthritis in his back, both back hips and all of his legs. After asking the opinion of the vet of how to treat Charlie and having Charlie in "doggie diapers" for three months and watching him cry when he went up and down the stairs, we finally decided that it was time to let him go. Charlie was 15 years old. But it was my loving husband who decided to give Charlie his "last supper", or breakfast as it may be. Bill got up and made a pan of brownies, bacon and eggs, biscuits, gravy, and sausage. We sat out on the patio and had breakfast with Charlie. We gave him one of our good plates, filled it with all the goodies and watched him enjoy every bite. He didn't know what was about to happen, but he so enjoyed the moment of being with us, outside where he loved to be, eating everything that he knew was too good to be true… especially the chocolate brownies!

Charlie has been gone now for some time. I don't know why this image has been so clear in mind lately, except that as I write it, I am reminded that Charlie lived every moment for the moment. He didn't think about "what is going to happen to me", he just loved the moment. So many times, I miss the moment, because I get so caught up in the "what if's", and "what now's". I could learn a lesson from my precious Charlie… live today for today.

In *Matthew 6: 25 Jesus tells us, "Do not worry about your life, what you will eat or drink, or about your body and what you will wear. Is not life more important than food, and the body more important than the clothes you wear?"* I hope as your day goes by, that you can see the moments of joy right before your eyes. Take a few moments and pass on your worries to God and let Him take care of you and enjoy the chocolate brownies of life.

Today enjoy the moment for the moment.

****

ASK YOURSELF:

What is God revealing to me today?

_____
_____
_____
_____
_____
_____
_____
_____
_____
_____

How do I see God working in my life today?

_____
_____
_____
_____
_____
_____
_____
_____
_____

What can I do to bring a blessing to someone else?

_____
_____
_____
_____
_____
_____
_____
_____
_____
_____

My daughter and I were driving down a country road and saw a field of beautiful horses. They all looked very happy and content, grazing on the green pasture. Then at the edge of the pasture there was one horse all alone with his head stretched out and bent down through the fence. As we got closer to this horse, we realized he had the barbed wire fence bent down and was trying to reach for the grass outside of the pasture. We have probably all seen the giraffe at the zoo, that has stretched his neck so far to reach "fresh food" because everything around him was dried hay or worn-down grass. Or the monkey who is reaching out of his cage to get that one blade of grass that is sprouting up out of the concrete. But why was this horse trying so hard to get something that he already had? Couldn't this horse see that he was standing in green pastures? Couldn't he see that the grass was the same on both sides of the fence? Why was he trying so hard to reach something that was right underneath his feet? Couldn't he be content with what was right before him?

Sometimes I am like this horse. I think that I need more, or that what God has given me isn't enough. Yet many times when I stretch out my neck to obtain something different, it doesn't make me any happier or content. Don't get me wrong, stretching out and reaching for higher goals in life is the way of life. We are to strive to be better people, but, while we are on the path to a different road, sometimes we have to be content for a while. I am not saying to be complacent, but to be content that God has us where we are for a reason. Philippians 4:11-12 says it like this: "…I have learned to be content, whatever the circumstance. I know what it is to be in need, and I know what it is to have plenty. I have learned the secret of being content in any and every situation, whether well fed or hungry, whether living in plenty or living in want. I can do everything through Him who gives me strength."

Today, stop and look around you and see if you are standing in a green pasture, and just breathe.

****

ASK YOURSELF:

What is God revealing to me today?

_____
_____
_____
_____
_____
_____
_____
_____
_____
_____

How do I see God working in my life today?

_____
_____
_____
_____
_____
_____
_____
_____
_____

What can I do to bring a blessing to someone else?

_____
_____
_____
_____
_____
_____
_____
_____

I took a trip to Canada. Specifically, St. John's, New Foundland. If you aren't sure where that is, pull out the map and look at the furthest most east point of Canada and there you will see New Foundland. Honestly, until I was asked to take the trip, I never really knew where New Foundland was. Since this was unfamiliar surroundings, it seemed logical to take the Tom-tom with me. These things are awesome. Just punch in the location of where you want to go, and a magic voice speaks through the device and leads you directly to where you want to be. Or does it?

One of the things that intrigues me when traveling, are the old churches, museums, and castles. There were amazing pictures found on the internet, of an old Church of Christ church built in the 1800's in St. John's. In my one-half day of leisure, the venture started… in goes the address of the church in St. John's. You can hear "her" voice, … "at the next intersection, turn left – go 1.5 miles – stay in the right lane – take a right in ½ mile – stay in the right lane – take the hwy for 2.2 miles – take the 282 exit – turn left…" on and on she keeps talking for about 30 minutes. Finally, the address is showing to be only ¾ of mile away, then ½ mile, then 2 minutes… and alas the Tom-tom makes the announcement – "you have reached your destination!" The destination was not exactly the right place. Tom-tom had led me to be parked in front of someone's home in an old neighborhood. It was a quaint home, but nonetheless it was not the oldest Church of Christ Church. How could that be? I did exactly what it told me to do… why in the world did I end up here?

It was clear, I followed something that I put my faith in, but it didn't really have the correct path. It was a couple of turns and stops off from where the church actually was. At that moment, I realized that I do the very same thing in life. How many times have I followed someone thinking that they had answers to questions that only God could answer? Or have trusted in a job or church to guide me and give me peace and comfort, only to find that they brought more questions and turmoil? People, jobs, and churches are necessary in our lives, but often we put all our trust and hope in those things first, and then we don't understand why we feel lost or abandoned by them. When we have followed those things, Christ reminds us that we can turn to Him who does have the direction to peace, joy and comfort. Jesus tells us clearly in John 10:27 - *"My sheep listen to my voice; I know them, and they follow Me. I give them eternal life and they will never perish; no one can snatch them out of My hand..."*

Wherever you are traveling today in this thing called life, remember to seek out the direction of the One who will always guide you in safety, comfort, and truth, and will bring you to a glorious destination.

****

ASK YOURSELF:

What is God revealing to me today?

_____
_____
_____
_____
_____
_____

How do I see God working in my life today?

_____
_____
_____
_____
_____
_____

What can I do to bring a blessing to someone else?

_____
_____
_____
_____
_____
_____

When was the last time that you went to an art gallery? My children are very creative and have a great ability to capture their love of life in their talents of drawing, painting, and photography, and have had several pieces of their work entered into art contests over the years and made it to the gallery.

Every time I go and look at the many different aspects of art, I am fascinated at how each piece is so individual. Each person that created their work, took time, effort, and exactness to make their masterpiece to look exactly like it looks. Every brush stroke is important, until the final one is placed, and the artist signs their name to the work. Every pencil line on the drawing, every piece of paper placed on the Mache', and the countless numbers of photographs until the perfect one is taken. Every piece has a beginning and an end, and along the way there are touch ups and re-dos and then suddenly, there it is .... the finished product!
Perfection at the end!

Do you know that you are the same way? Every day is a new stroke of the brush by God. He is preparing you for the perfection that HE sees in you.
Philippians 1:6 tells us, "He who began a good work in you, will see it to completion until the day of Jesus Christ." You see, God started his good work with you the day you were being formed in your mother's womb, and each day He places one more pencil line, one more brush stroke, one more polishing of the silver until your day of completion, which will be when we are facing Christ. We are all in the place of being formed for the perfection of Him. That's it. Nothing more, nothing less. We are being placed here on earth by Him to share about HIS perfection, not ours.

Today you may not be perfect but know that you are being painted on. What a beautiful picture God is painting as HE paints you! He has signed His name on you because YOU are His masterpiece!

****

ASK YOURSELF:

What is God revealing to me today?

_____
_____
_____
_____
_____
_____
_____
_____
_____
_____

How do I see God working in my life today?

_____
_____
_____
_____
_____
_____
_____
_____
_____

What can I do to bring a blessing to someone else?

_____
_____
_____
_____
_____
_____
_____
_____
_____

Journey Date 59_____

I don't know about you, but I love to start new projects. For me, it would be projects like sewing curtains, or making a costume, or a crafty project. I usually get these kinds of projects finished, I know what I am trying to accomplish, so I work until I get the project done. Then there are the "house" projects. I can honestly say that our household probably falls in the 90% of red-blooded Americans that start a house project, with good intentions of course, and get about 80% done. Let's see, like wall papering the kitchen and putting up new chair rail boards. The old paper comes down, (that takes a while), the new paper goes up (that takes a little while longer), then the trim boards need to be painted, cut to fit the wall, and nailed up. This is where I would probably get stuck. If enough time goes by, I may eventually just say, "oh we don't need those boards up there anyway", even though the boards are laying in the garage waiting to be painted. There is just something about "putting off 'till tomorrow, and tomorrow and tomorrow…."

Have you ever felt like "you" were the project. Need to lose weight, quit smoking, exercise more, stop watching so much television, read more, pray more, be nicer… the list could on and on. I can tell you that no matter what kind of problem or "project" that you think "you" have to fix, is already taken care of. *Phillipians 1:6 tells us, "being confident of the very thing that HE who has begun a good work in you, _____, will complete it until the day of Jesus Christ."*

What an awesome vision for you and me. Read this verse again but put your name in the blank. God is not finished with you yet. He started a "project" a long time ago and HE will complete it. You may try your hardest to make things right, but God is the finisher of the project. He started it. He will finish it. He never leaves a project incomplete. Isn't that great news for us!

Today I hope that you will know that God has great plans for you and that you are a good work that He created.

****

ASK YOURSELF:

What is God revealing to me today?

_____
_____
_____
_____
_____
_____
_____
_____
_____
_____

How do I see God working in my life today?

_____
_____
_____
_____
_____
_____
_____
_____

What can I do to bring a blessing to someone else?

_____
_____
_____
_____
_____
_____
_____
_____

Journey Date 60_____

"I would sooner live in a cottage and wonder at everything, than live in a castle and wonder at nothing." - Quote by: Joan Winmill Brown

What type of house do you live in? Is it a huge house with several bedrooms, or is it a small apartment with just enough space to put everything you have in it? Or possibly a simple three-bedroom, brick house in a quiet neighborhood, or maybe even in a hut in Africa. Some people are living in tents and cardboard boxes. Personally, I live in a double-wide mobile home. Many people call them "trailers", others call it a "modular house". What I call it is "home".   I read the quote above by Joan Brown and immediately thought this is exactly where I want to be. I don't want to miss out on the wonders of life.

The ultimate home that I want to live in is God's home. But, on the way I don't want to miss out on anything that HE puts before me. Sometimes the "things" that we live for, or work for get in the way of God's wonders. I know there are so many obstacles that can stop us along the way, but the "wonders" that are in front of us are just as many.   Just this afternoon while I was outside grilling burgers, I looked over and sitting on top of my crepe' myrtle was a baby bird. He appeared to be a "youngster". Probably just pushed out of the tree because he looked so terrified. For half an hour or so I watched this little fellow, and he didn't move. What made that little baby bird sit in the tree right next to my patio? Why didn't the baby fly away? I believe it was one of God's wonders staring me right in the face. It was so small I almost missed it, but HE opened my eyes to see a marvelous sight.

What are you living for? Are you living for God's ultimate home, looking for His wonders along the way? Or are you living day to day, in dread and suffocation of this world's stuff? Jesus gives comfort to the disciples in John 14: 1-4 - *"Do not let your hearts be troubled. Trust in God; trust also in Me. In My Father's house are many rooms; if it were not so, I would have told you. And if I go and prepare a place for you, I will come back and take you to be with Me that you also may be where I am. You know the way to the place I am going."* Isn't that wonderful, our Savior instructs us not to be troubled, because one day we will live in God's Mansion.

Today, remember to search for the wonders of life along the way.

****

ASK YOURSELF:

What is God revealing to me today?

_____
_____
_____
_____
_____
_____
_____

How do I see God working in my life today?

_____
_____
_____
_____
_____
_____
_____

What can I do to bring a blessing to someone else?

_____
_____
_____
_____
_____
_____
_____

Journey Day 61 _____

A question was posed to me this week ..." What is God's call for your life?" Is that a tough question for you, as it was for me? When we are younger, we may think that when we "grow up", we will become "somebody" or accomplish something that is amazing. We have our idea of who we think we should marry, and where we should live and how many kids we will have, if any. We feel like the world is just at our fingertips and that we can accomplish anything. As a matter of fact, the Baby Boomer group told their children (this includes me) that they could do or be whatever they wanted. (Which really is not true, have you ever seen a 7-foot jockey?) Don't misunderstand me, we strive to be the best we can be, but what is the call on our life? We may even invent something that would impact the world, kind of like Facebook. So, do you think that Mark Zuckerberg ever thought that he would be the youngest billionaire in the world? As a kid, did he dream or believe that he would have created something that has allowed communication across the world from old to new friends? And now where is he, do you think he is happy? Very wealthy of course, but was Facebook the only "call" on his life?

Well, we do grow older, and what we dreamed of when we were younger may not have happened. Or, maybe it did happen, but then, it got interrupted by a tragedy or difficult situation like a divorce, loss of a job, car accident, severe illness, chronic pain, or possibly the death of loved one. Are these really things that are in the "call" of our life? I don't have an answer for that question. That is a question that has to be asked of God. But I do know that He does "call" us to be His and to remember that no matter where we stand or what we are going through that HE always stands with us. Jeremiah 29:11-14 is very clear. This is what the Lord says, "I know the plans I have for you _____, plans to prosper you and not to harm you, plans to give you hope and a future. Then you will call on Me and pray to Me, and I WILL listen to you. You will seek Me and find Me when you seek Me with all your heart, I will be found by you."

Do you know what God has called you to do in life? Honestly, that is still a question that is difficult for me to answer. My prayer is that I would listen and follow where He leads and that every day I live, I live to fulfill the call on my life, and that is to be a woman of faith.

Today, if you are wondering what the call is on your life, just ask Him, He is ready and waiting to listen.

****

ASK YOURSELF:

What is God revealing to me today?

_____
_____
_____
_____
_____
_____
_____

How do I see God working in my life today?

_____
_____
_____
_____
_____
_____
_____

What can I do to bring a blessing to someone else?

_____
_____
_____
_____
_____
_____
_____

Journey Day 62 _____

When my son was in Afghanistan. I would a box of goodies to him each week or so. But the last box I sent I wanted to put an anniversary card in it, as he would celebrate his 1st Anniversary on 5/12/12. The cool thing about the large flat rate box at the post office, is that no matter how much it weighs, it always costs the same amount. With great efforts I packed the box to its capacity. I taped the box, with duct tape (he loves duct tape) and clear shipping tape. It was sealed tight, and nothing else was getting in that box. I wrote his address on the outside of the box, filled out the form and set it on the counter, ready to mail. Then as I turned from the table, I remembered …. I forgot to put the card in the box. Did I really want to unseal the box? All the work to get it crammed full and sealed shut. I decided not to unseal it, but to mail the card separately and to go ahead and mail the box like it was.

Did you know that God does the same kind of thing with us?   Let me show you how I know…
Ephesians 1:13 and 14- *"In Him you also trusted after you heard the word of truth, the gospel of your salvation; in whom also, having believed, you were sealed with the Holy Spirit of promise, who is the guarantee of our inheritance until the redemption of the purchased possession to the praise of HIS glory."*

Isn't that something – He "seals" us with Himself, the Holy Spirit, and we are guaranteed to live in His kingdom forever. All we have to put in our "box" is the word of truth, and our salvation and it is a guarantee that we are "sealed", and no one can "un-seal" us. Not even ourselves. Circumstances may seem difficult and hopeless and look like the "seal" has been broken and "other things" are trying to be "stuffed" into the box… but this is God's promise… WE ARE SEALED!!!

I pray today that God would fill you with an abundance of His Holy Spirit, to guide you, to hold you, to give you hope but most of all to show you how much you are loved.

****

ASK YOURSELF:

What is God revealing to me today?

_____
_____
_____
_____
_____
_____
_____
_____
_____
_____
_____

How do I see God working in my life today?

_____
_____
_____
_____
_____
_____
_____
_____
_____

What can I do to bring a blessing to someone else?

_____
_____
_____
_____
_____
_____
_____
_____
_____
_____

Journey Day 63 _____

This has been a very challenging day. I went to the funeral of a precious 9-year-old little girl. She was the niece of a friend of mine. There are no words that really can express the heartfelt pain of this family. So many questions running through my mind, I can't even begin to imagine what is going through theirs. When my father breathed his last breath of air at the age of 81, it made more sense than for this little one to breathe her last breath. My dad accomplished much in his life, had a huge family, left many great memories behind. The work that the Father started in my dad was finished… you could say "the construction was complete". There wasn't anything else that my dad had to do, nor anything else that the Lord wanted to accomplish in his life. Dad had everything in order and was "ready" to go to Heaven. Don't misunderstand me, I miss my dad every day, and there doesn't seem to be a week that goes by that I don't shed tears, but this sweet little girl, to be taken to Heaven with so much life yet to live…it just doesn't make sense to me. Was the "construction complete" in her young life?

Right now, there seems to be more questions than answers.

The Lord tells us that He "knit us in our mother's womb and knows every cell in our bodies", which means He created this precious one, and He has called her home to Heaven.

"Today" is a little different, would you stop for just a moment and pray for this family or for any family that has lost a loved one recently. Even in our doubt and confusion, He hears our prayers and wants to bring comfort and peace.

****

ASK YOURSELF:

What is God revealing to me today?

_____
_____
_____
_____
_____
_____
_____
_____
_____

How do I see God working in my life today?

_____
_____
_____
_____
_____
_____
_____
_____
_____

What can I do to bring a blessing to someone else?

_____
_____
_____
_____
_____
_____
_____
_____
_____

Journey Day 64 _____

On Father's Day, that meant we were going to grill steak on the "barby". Though it was a special day for my husband, he was still the one who cooked the steak. He always seems to get them just right. One of the things I love about summer and grilling outside is the aroma of the meat searing on the grill. It doesn't matter what kind of meat it is; the smell is so enticing and really makes my mouth water. What's funny about this is typically red meat is not my usual preference. Fish, or chicken or even a good salad, is what pleases my tummy. But there is just something about the billowing smoke from the grill that makes my mouth water and causes a longing for a slab of some type of red meat.

Our pastor was talking about the "perfect" sacrifice that the Israelites were to give to God. They were to sacrifice their best animal, and it would be pleasing to the Lord. This is not something new to me but hearing it again gave me a whole new perspective. If we are to love what the Lord loves, then it would make sense why that searing smell of the meat is so enticing. It is something that is pleasing to God, and if I am to be more like Him and less like me, then it only makes sense that it would be pleasing to me. This may sound kind strange but let me write out what Paul says to the Ephesians…" Be imitators of God, therefore, as dearly loved children, and live a life of love, just as Christ loved us and He gave Himself up for us as a fragrant offering and sacrifice to God." – Ephesians 5:1 & 2

You see as we walk closer with God, we watch what God does, which is to mostly love us. When we stay in that closeness, we learn to love like He does, and we learn how much Christ loved us. His love was not cautious but extravagant. He didn't love us to get something from us, but to give everything of Himself to us, by offering His life. This is how we are to love others. When giving of ourselves without expectation then the air is filled with the sweet aroma of our Lord.

Today, I hope that you will love someone without expectation. In return you will be loved by our amazing God who will fill your heart with more than you can imagine and fill the air with the sweet aroma of His goodness.

****

ASK YOURSELF:

What is God revealing to me today?

_____
_____
_____
_____
_____
_____
_____
_____
_____
_____

How do I see God working in my life today?

_____
_____
_____
_____
_____
_____
_____
_____

What can I do to bring a blessing to someone else?

_____
_____
_____
_____
_____
_____
_____
_____
_____

Journey Day 65 _____

A dear friend came back into my life after several years. Before I met up with my friend, I had great anticipation of excitement, wondering how much each of us had changed, and then I realized how much I missed talking with him. I remembered how he searched for truth and hungered for wisdom. I forgot how much our conversation's brought deeper insight to who each of us were on the inside. But most of all I forgot that he had a great listening ear, and a voice to share encouragement. Then I realized as I was getting in my car and my husband was getting in his car, and my friend was leaving, that I had missed out on a whole lot of sharing and caring over the past few years. Why did I wait these years to see my friend? Why did I let time steal away such a precious commodity of caring?

Then I understood, it isn't that I didn't want to visit with my friend, I just didn't do it. I made excuses. "Life" got too busy --- and there it was --- I do the very same thing with God and Jesus. So many things that I let get in the way with my "time" with "my friend". The closest friend I could ever have, Jesus! Yet, I let time pass me by and ask those questions, like "Lord, what ARE you doing in my life?" and there He is ready to answer me, I have to ask and then listen. Jesus is always ready to show up at the next meeting, whenever that meeting is. Three years, three months, three weeks, three days, three hours, three minutes.... It really doesn't matter to Him; He always shows up with the answer. Just pray!

Luke 3:21 & 22 says: "When all the people were baptized, Jesus was baptized too. And as He was praying, Heaven was opened, and the Holy Spirit descended on Him in bodily form like a dove. And a voice came from Heaven: "You are My Son, whom I love; with You I am well pleased.""

Isn't that awesome! All Jesus did was pray and Heaven was opened! All we must do is pray and Heaven will open! *Thank You Lord today for Your inspiring words and Your unending love. Thank You Lord for my husband and my friend with whom I could share, and they could share with me about You. Thank You Lord that the Heavens will open when we call on Your name. I love You!"*

May you call out to Him today and the Heavens open up before you.

****

ASK YOURSELF:

What is God revealing to me today?

_____
_____
_____
_____
_____
_____
_____
_____
_____
_____

How do I see God working in my life today?

_____
_____
_____
_____
_____
_____
_____
_____

What can I do to bring a blessing to someone else?

_____
_____
_____
_____
_____
_____
_____

Over the weekend I made some chocolate fudge cupcakes. I coaxed my sister into giving me her secret recipe for her amazing dark chocolate fudge cake. (It IS the best!) So, I followed the recipe, and poured all the cupcake holders with the batter. It looked right, it poured right, it even tasted right (yep, I had to lick the bowl). They were ready to go, and I was excited to see if I could have replicated her wonderful cake. So, I head over to the oven, open the door and the oven is stone cold. Now what was I going to do. I had 30 cupcake tins filled and needed to get these things cooked. I crawled on the floor, looked in the bottom of the oven and sure enough, the pilot light was out. So, I got a long match, lit the pilot, turned the oven on, we were back in business… so I thought.

It was about 9:30 at night when all of this was taking place. I was getting tired and wanted to get these cupcakes in the oven, but I had to wait for the heat to rise to the right temperature. After waiting about 15 to 20 minutes, I decided to put the cupcakes in the oven. Surely it must have been at 345 degrees by now. Probably 10 minutes after I put them in, I could smell the cupcakes cooking, but it wasn't a pleasant smell, more like chocolate on fire with a little charcoal on the side. I opened the oven door to find that the cupcakes had expanded well over the pan and was pouring over the sides. After the pan was pulled out of the oven, I could see the center of these so-called cupcakes was sunken and raw. What a mess they turned out to be. It was so upsetting to see such a sight. I knew I should have waited. Why did I have to hurry to get these in the oven? Why did I let my tiredness take control of me? Why didn't I wait?

There are times that I am this way with the Lord also. I want to "hurry Him up" with the answer that I am waiting for. Doesn't He know what I want? Doesn't He hear my heart cry of pain and sorrow? What is taking Him so long to help me with my marriage, or my job, or loss of job? Or you may be asking, does He really know how broken I feel now that I am alone? Didn't he see that argument that I got in to with my best friend? And the grieving that I am going through at the loss of my parent, can't He make that go away? If the answer doesn't come quickly, then we may think that He doesn't hear us.

Psalm 40 is a great answer to whether God hears us, and whether He thinks that we are important to Him. *"I waited patiently for the Lord; He turned to me and heard my cry. He lifted me out of the slimy pit, out of the mud and mire; He set my feet on a rock and gave me a firm place to stand. He put a new song in my mouth…"*
Yes, it can be hard to wait. But when we do wait, the Lord fills our heart with a new song of joy, and tenderly tells us "I do hear you".

Waiting seems to be one of the hardest words in the dictionary for mankind to desire. But, oh if you are a believer in Christ, know that HE, is preparing a place for you to never have to worry again. If you do not know the Lord Jesus Christ as your Savior, He is waiting for you right now.

****

ASK YOURSELF:

What is God revealing to me today?

_____
_____
_____
_____
_____

How do I see God working in my life today?

_____
_____
_____
_____

What can I do to bring a blessing to someone else?

_____
_____
_____
_____

Journey Day 67 _____

Does anyone out there have a shirt, or pants or some type of clothing that is your absolute favorite? There is one t-shirt that I have that has become my favorite. It's the one shirt that I wanted to wear every weekend. I got the shirt while my son was in Afghanistan. It was from an organization called "Soldiers Angels". There's nothing fancy about it. It's a white t-shirt with the Soldiers Angels logo on the back, and the front side has "boot prints" with the saying, "May no soldier walk alone." While eating yummy spaghetti one night, some of the sauce splashed on the front of my shirt. Before it got to set in, I took the shirt off and I covered the spot with Spray 'n Wash, and threw it in the washer. After washing for 20 minutes, I pulled the shirt out, and the stain had already set in. So, I used something a little stronger, Oxy Clean Gel. This stuff is great, it takes out everything. So, I washed it again…. And of course, the stain did not come out. So, for a third try I used Oxy Clean powder and made a paste and put it on the spot. Surely this must work… Nope, the stain was fading, but there was still a slight hint of color. Okay, this meant war. That stain was NOT going to stay on my favorite shirt. So, if you haven't guessed by now, I put all three things on the spot at one time. I sprayed the Spray 'N Wash, then pressed on the Oxy Clean Gel, and then poured on the Oxy Clean powder. If this didn't work, I was going to give up. It worked! The stain was finally gone.

This made me think that we are a lot like this shirt. God looks down on His children and says to each of them, "You are my favorite". Then as time goes on, there are things that we might do that we think could cause a "stain" in our lives. Possibly a "stain" that is so bad, that we know it will remain forever. Or even something that caused a "stain" from long ago, and because it has been a part of our lives for so long, we know there is nothing that can get that one clean. Each of us has those "stains". They have different names; drugs, alcohol, abuse, neglect, abortion, affairs, theft, cutting and the list could go on and on. Only you and God know what that "stain" is in your life. The great thing is that God gives us a way to get the stain out, and that is through His Son Christ. But we not only get it through Christ, but we also get it through God Himself and through His Holy Spirit. Just like the three things above, God gives us Himself in three different ways to remove the "stain".

Psalm 51 says it like this: "Have mercy on me, O God, according to your unfailing love; according to your great compassion, blot out my transgressions. Wash away all of my "stains" and cleanse me from my sin" ... "Cleanse me with a gentle fragrance, and I will be clean; wash me, and I will be whiter than snow."

Today, if there is a "stain" in your life that you feel you will never be cleansed from, call out to God the Father, Christ the Son, and the Holy Spirit, and watch what will happen. God still says, "Child you are my favorite."

****

ASK YOURSELF:

What is God revealing to me today?

_____
_____
_____
_____
_____
_____

How do I see God working in my life today?

_____
_____
_____
_____
_____
_____
_____

What can I do to bring a blessing to someone else?

_____
_____
_____
_____
_____

Journey Day 68 _____

Animals are quite entertaining. Whether you have a cat, a dog, a horse, or whatever it is that you have, you probably know their method of communication. I'm not talking about the everyday "meow" or the wag of a tail from the dog. I am talking about that place of communication where your pet is REALLY trying to get your attention. Our cat, Samson, was wondering around the house just meowing at the top of his little lungs. After listening to him for some time, I decided to go where he was and see if I could figure out what he wanted. "Do you want food?", even though there was food in the bowl. "How about water, do you want some water?" I went to both water bowls, and they were filled to the rim. What did he want? I sat on the bed and asked him again, "what do you want?" He jumped up on the bed and sat next to me and meowed. He rubbed his head on my arm, to give me a little nudge and then I figured it out. He wanted someone to scratch behind his ears. I was trying to listen to what he wanted but needed his help to completely understand. He was very content and happy when I began petting him.

Many times, I cry out, and wonder around, and feel like no one is listening to me. Do you know that feeling? The days or weeks or even months are filled with painful situations and difficult decisions, and you just want someone to really listen to you. The "food bowl" is full, and the "water bowl" has water, but there is so much more that is burdening your heart, that food and water just won't satisfy the need. We want someone to listen and to bring comfort. We desire to sit close to someone. So close that you don't even have to say anything, but they just know what you need. Psalm 34 tells us that when we cry out, God listens: "Is anyone crying for help? God is listening ready to rescue you. If your heart is broken, you'll find God right there. The Lord is close to the brokenhearted and saves those who are crushed in spirit".

Today, are you crying out for help, and still feel that no one is listening? God is always ready to listen and bring comfort. Call on His name, and He will be by your side.

****

ASK YOURSELF:

What is God revealing to me today?

_____
_____
_____
_____
_____
_____
_____
_____
_____
_____

How do I see God working in my life today?

_____
_____
_____
_____
_____
_____
_____
_____
_____
_____

What can I do to bring a blessing to someone else?

_____
_____
_____
_____
_____
_____
_____
_____
_____
_____

Journey Day 69 _____

How many times in our lives do we "wish" things would be different? We say the "if only's" – but we know that the "if only's" really aren't the reasons we are where we are. Certainly, we make choices and circumstances happen, but I believe there is more than the choices that we make - it's what we do after the choices are made. I heard someone say that we often make choices, but fall back into the old patterns or ways that we were once in. Think of it this way– if you were stuck in a deep gully or a rut alongside a road, and you wonder how will you get out? Then you decide to climb, and dig foot holes in the dirt, to get out. You grasp onto the rocks and roots in the dirt and finally get out of the rut and you are standing on the edge of higher ground. It is so refreshing to look out across the road, then to look farther and see the vast land, and it feels good to know that there is a new place to go. There is a new path to walk down. Then, a little fear sets in, and uncertainty of what is out there, so you take a step back, and you fall back into the rut. Only to find yourself back in the same place.

My friend, I've realized that once you have stepped onto new and higher ground, we should quickly turn around and face the rut, and take note of where we came from – but not step back into it. We should pick up a shovel and fill in that rut with "dirt, rocks, and soil", which could be new thoughts, ideas, and plans. When we change our thoughts or actions, we step into a new place, and we will no longer fall back into the rut. It becomes a new ground to get us to the next place in life.

We all have the "ruts", whether it is a relationship, a job, even a passion that has died. Today my friend, my prayer is that you have the courage to climb out and see the new road ahead of you.

Strength today comes from the very familiar passage of Psalm 23. Let me write it out as written in The Message: *"God, my Shepherd, I don't need a thing. You have bedded me down in lush meadows. You find me quiet pools to drink from. True to Your word, You let me catch my breath and send me in the right direction. Even when the way goes through Death Valley, I am not afraid when You walk at my side. Your trusty shepherds crook makes me feel secure. You serve me a six-course dinner right in front of my enemies. You revive my drooping head; my cup brims with blessing. Your beauty and love chase after me every day of my life. I'm back home in the house of God for the rest of my life."*

May you reach out to Him today and travel down the pathway that is fresh and new.

****

ASK YOURSELF:

What is God revealing to me today?

_____
_____
_____
_____
_____
_____
_____

How do I see God working in my life today?

_____
_____
_____
_____
_____
_____
_____

What can I do to bring a blessing to someone else?

_____
_____
_____
_____
_____
_____
_____

Journey Day 70 _____

I have a friend whose son and daughter-in-law just had their first baby. Many of us have experienced childbirth and it is one of the most wonderful things that can happen in a persons' life. But I want to share about the labor pains of this woman. Since this was her first, it was a little frightening and uncertain of exactly how she was supposed to feel. Fortunately, this young lady had a wonderful nurse. The nurse was small in stature and stood just about face to face with the young lady who was in labor. The nurse would "coach" her and tell her "Okay, just breathe slow breaths – now relax". It was comforting for the young woman to see the nurses face while she was having contractions. Of course, as busy as hospitals get, the nurse would be called out of the room, only to leave the young woman with her towering husband. He was a wonderful husband and trying to be as comforting as he could be. He took the direction that the nurse was going and would say, "okay honey, just breathe – now relax". But he didn't have quite the same effect on the young woman, as the nurse had with her.

The nurse would come back into the room and look at the young woman face to face and calmly say "just breathe, you are doing good", then the labor would subside, and everything was calm. Then, the nurse would leave again. And here comes more labor pain, and the tall, handsome man steps up to be the caring husband, but could see his wife was not comforted. Then during the intense and difficult labor, the young woman reaches up and grabs her husbands' face with her two hands and pulls him down to her and says, "down here, I need to see your face down here where I am." He understood exactly what she was saying, and he knelt to be by her side, and "coached" her at her level. Then, she felt his comfort and peace.

What an amazing picture of what I believe that God wants us to do with Him. When we are in that place that seems so intense and difficult, and the answer does not appear to be within reach, we should cry out to Him and say, "down here Lord, I need you down here with me". Then we reach out our hands and fall to our knees and He meets us right in that place. We don't have to say much because He is ready to come and meet us right where we are.

Psalm 18 tells us how David cried out to God: *"I love you God! The Lord is my rock, my fortress, and my deliverer; God is the place that I can take refuge...In my distress I called to the Lord, I cried to my God for help. From His temple He heard my voice; my cry came before Him, into His ears.... Then He reached down from on high and took hold of me; He drew me out of deep waters..."*

What is your "labor pain" today? Is it a struggle in your work environment, or do you have a difficult decision to make that doesn't seem to have a clear answer. Possibly you are concerned for your financial welfare, or the economy of the world. Or maybe medical tests results are not that favorable. Whatever the pains are, as you call out His name, He comes and kneels right beside you, and will catch every tear, hear every sigh and touch your heart gently.

****

ASK YOURSELF:

What is God revealing to me today?

_____
_____
_____
_____

How do I see God working in my life today?

_____
_____
_____
_____

What can I do to bring a blessing to someone else?

_____
_____
_____
_____
_____

After reading these life stories, I have one question left – do you know Jesus?

The Word tells us that all have sinned and fall short of the glory of God and are justified freely by His grace through the redemption that came by Christ Jesus. God sacrificed Jesus on the altar of the world to clear the world of sin. Having faith in Him sets us in the clear. God decided on this course of action in full view of the public – to set the world in the clear with Himself through the sacrifice of Jesus, finally taking care of the sins He had so patiently endured. This is not only clear, but it's now – this is current history! God sets things right. He also makes it possible for us to live in His rightness.

If you have never asked Jesus to come into your heart, pray this simple prayer:

"Jesus, forgive me, for I am a sinner. Come into my heart and lead me each day of my life. Thank You Jesus for loving me so much that you would sacrifice Your life for me. I am Yours and You are mine today and through all eternity. Amen."

If you prayed this prayer, tell someone. Or send an email to **today@prodigalpublishing.com** and we will celebrate with you.

All praises to our King!

"But encourage one another daily, as long as it called _Today_, so that none of you may be hardened by sin's deceitfulness."- Hebrews 3:13.

Made in the USA
Columbia, SC
13 October 2022